GREAT SHIPWRECKS
of the
MAINE COAST

Great Shipwrecks of the Maine Coast

Jeremy D'Entremont

To Marlene + Jack —
Smooth Sailing!
Best Wishes.

6/25/19

Commonwealth Editions
Carlisle, Massachusetts

ISBN 978-0-9819430-6-0

Library of Congress Cataloging-in-Publication Data
D'Entremont, Jeremy.
Great shipwrecks of the Maine coast / Jeremy D'Entremont.
p. cm.
Includes bibliographical references.
ISBN 978-0-9819430-6-0 (alk. paper)
1. Shipwrecks—Maine—Atlantic Coast—History. 2. Atlantic Coast (Me.)—
History—Anecdotes. 3. Maine—History—Anecdotes. I. Title.
F19.6.D46 2010
910.9163'4—dc22   2010005006

Cover design by John Barnett / 4 Eyes Design
Interior design by Joyce C. Weston

Published by Commonwealth Editions,
an imprint of Applewood Books
Carlisle, Massachusetts 01741
www.commonwealtheditions.com

Commonwealth Editions publishes books about the history, traditions,
and beauty of places in New England and throughout America
for adults and children.

To request a free copy of our current print catalog
featuring our best-selling books, write to:
Applewood Books
P.O. Box 27
Carlisle, MA 01741

MANUFACTURED IN THE UNITED STATES OF AMERICA

Contents

~ Contents ~

Introduction

FOR DIVERS and marine archaeologists, the appeal of shipwrecks is straightforward. Wrecks are like submerged time machines, windows to another world. The study of wrecks and the artifacts they hold can tell us much about the way ships were built and about the cultures that produced them.

But what's the attraction for the rest of us? Why do people flock to a beach when the bones of an ancient wreck show themselves after a storm? And why have shipwrecks been the source of so much popular art and literature through the centuries?

A chief reason is that shipwrecks represent a pure, primal form of human drama. It's a cliché to say that disasters bring out the best and worst in people, but it's also absolutely true. Extremes of human behavior, from the basest cowardice to the most selfless heroism, are often on exhibit in the same story. Given the intense physical and emotional stress produced by a shipwreck, flight and fight are two sides of the same coin.

One of the best maritime authors, John Rousmaniere, has written, "Few events can thrash a life—or glorify it—as effectively as a storm at sea." Shipwrecks caused by weather serve as rude reminders that our modern technology hasn't given us mastery over our oceans. As Lord Byron wrote in *The Dark, Blue Sea*, "Man marks the earth with ruin, but his control stops with the shore."

In the case of many shipwrecks, there's also great mystery involved. When there are no survivors to provide witness, careful detective work can sometimes give us an idea of what happened. We can rarely know the whole story with any certainty; the 1941 loss of the *Don* in Casco Bay is a prime example. But we can speculate, always a popular human pastime.

The United Nations estimates that 3 million shipwrecks litter our ocean floors. Maine can't boast as many wrecks—if that's something to boast about—as the Outer Banks of North Carolina, Nova Scotia's Sable Island, or Cape Cod. But with about 3,500 miles of coastline (more than California) and more than 2,000 islands, there have been plenty of disasters. According to National Oceanic and Atmospheric Administration's Office of Coast Survey, there are over seven hundred known wrecks in the Gulf of Maine, which extends from Saint John, New Brunswick, to the Nantucket Shoals.

It would be impossible to include information on every maritime disaster on the coast of Maine in any single volume, but I apologize if a particular wreck that's of special interest to you is not included here. I've presented a "greatest hits" (no pun intended) collection here, focusing on the most celebrated and dramatic stories. The final chapter includes quick synopses of many additional wrecks.

I should mention that the 1898 wreck of the steamer *Portland*—possibly New England's most famous shipwreck—isn't included because its final voyage began in Maine but ended in Massachusetts waters.

My personal fascination with maritime disasters has its roots in my childhood in the 1960s, when I enjoyed hearing the popular historian Edward Rowe Snow (1902–82) spin his salty yarns on Boston television and radio. In Snow's dramatic storytelling, storms, shipwrecks, pirates, and treasure were all stirred into a rich chowder that left me hungry for more.

I'm deeply indebted to Snow and the other authors who have sailed these waters before me, particularly Peter Dow Bachelder, whose *Shipwrecks and Maritime Disasters of the Maine Coast* is comprehensive and compelling.

This year we observe the three hundredth anniversary of the tragic wreck of the *Nottingham Galley* at Boon Island, and Kenneth Roberts's novel *Boon Island* remains an eminently readable account of a staggeringly harrowing story of survival.

Stephen Puleo's *Due to Enemy Action,* a gripping account of the sinking of the USS *Eagle 56* at the close of World War II, is an inspiration not just because of the emotional story it tells, but also for the depth of Puleo's research and commitment.

Warren C. Riess's *Angel Gabriel: The Elusive English Galleon* and Stacy L. Welner's *Tragedy in Casco Bay*, about the 1941 *Don* tragedy, deserve special mention as the best sources on those wrecks. George E. Buker's *The Penobscot Expedition* is a thorough telling of a dark but fascinating episode in American military history.

I wish to thank the Maine Historical Society, the Museum at Portland Head Light, the Vinalhaven Historical Society, and all the organizations and institutions that provided information and photos for this book. My sincere thanks once again to Commonwealth Editions, whose staff and consultants always help to make the process of writing and publishing a book a pleasure.

My wife, Charlotte Raczkowski, deserves my gratitude for her constant and patient support. My brother, Jim, is a writer whose work I greatly admire. He's encouraged my work and has always been more than willing to lend a helpful hand and moral support. I dedicate this book to him.

Jeremy D'Entremont
Portsmouth, New Hampshire
January 2010

CHAPTER ONE

The *Angel Gabriel* and the *James* in the Great Hurricane of 1635

METEOROLOGISTS categorize the August 1635 tempest that swept New England as one of five intense (category 3 or greater) hurricanes that have made landfall in the region in recorded history. In his journal William Bradford, governor of the Plymouth Colony in Massachusetts, described the hurricane as "such a mighty storm of wind and rain as none living in these parts, either English or Indians, ever saw." Despite the passing of nearly four centuries, we can piece together a vivid picture of this wildly destructive storm from Bradford's and several other eyewitnesses' accounts.

The storm followed a route that skirted the Virginia coast near Jamestown. Its center eventually crossed eastern Long Island and then careened into Narragansett Bay in Rhode Island. There it caused the tide to rise fourteen feet above normal and "drowned eight Indians flying from their wigwams," according to John Winthrop, of the Massachusetts Bay Colony.

The storm then passed between Plymouth and Boston. "It blew down many hundred thousands of trees," Bradford recorded, "turning up the stronger by the roots and breaking the higher pine trees off in the middle." Winthrop wrote that the gale "blew with such violence, with abundance of rain, that it blew down many hundreds of trees, near the towns, overthrew some houses, and drove the ships from their anchors." The English ship *Great Hope* was driven ashore at Charlestown, Massachusetts.

The hurricane apparently spawned a tornado in northeastern

Massachusetts. In his history of Newbury, Joshua Coffin wrote: "About eight o'clock there was in Salisbury and part of Amesbury the most violent tornado, or short hurricane, perhaps ever known in the country. It continued about three minutes, in which time it damaged, or entirely prostrated, nearly two hundred buildings. It removed two vessels, one of them of ninety tons, twenty-two feet from the stocks. The vein of the tempest was about a quarter of a mile in width on the river and about a mile and a half in length."

The damage along the coast and inland was comparable to that inflicted by the devastating hurricane of 1938, New England's most destructive twentieth-century storm. According to Brian Jarvinen of the National Hurricane Center, the 1635 storm was "probably the most intense hurricane in New England history."

It was certainly the worst storm encountered by New England's colonial settlers. It's believed that the winds reached 130 miles per hour, and the storm surge crested at twenty-one feet in Buzzards Bay. As Nicholas K. Coch, a hurricane expert, has observed, "The settlers easily could have packed up and gone home."

Along with the writings of Bradford and Winthrop, much of our knowledge of the gale comes from contemporary descriptions of two shipwrecks and one near miss: the *Watch and Wait* off Cape Ann, Massachusetts, the *Angel Gabriel* off Maine's Pemaquid Point, and the *James* at the Isles of Shoals.

The pinnace *Watch and Wait*, on its way to Marblehead from Ipswich, was wrecked in the storm on an island off Cape Ann, Massachusetts. Anthony Thacher later described the dreadful disaster:

> For on the 14th of this August, 1635, about ten at night, having a fresh gale of wind, our sails, being old and done, were split. The mariners, because that it was night, would not put to new sails, but resolved to cast anchor till the morning. But before daylight it pleased the Lord to send so mighty a storm, as the like was never known in New England since the English came, nor in the memory of any of the Indians. It was so furious, that our anchor came home. Whereupon the mariners let out more cable, which at last slipped away. Then our sailors knew not what to do, but we were driven before the wind and waves. . . .

Now look with me upon our distress, and consider of my misery, who beheld the ship broken, the water in her, and violently overwhelming us, my goods and provisions swimming in the seas, my friends almost drowned, and mine own poor children so untimely (if I may so term it without offence), before mine eyes drowned, and ready to be swallowed up, and dashed to pieces against the rocks by the merciless waves, and myself ready to accompany them.

Thacher and his wife, Elizabeth, were the only survivors of the wreck, in which twenty-one people died. John Greenleaf Whittier immortalized the disaster in his poem "The Swan Song of Parson Avery," and Thacher Island, home to twin lighthouses since 1771, owes its name to Anthony Thacher. A few years later, Thacher became one of the founding fathers of Yarmouth, Massachusetts.

The hurricane had lost little of its potency by the time it reached the coast of Maine, where two English ships, the *James* and the *Angel Gabriel,* had just finished crossing the Atlantic. The Reverend Richard Mather (1596–1669), who later became the father of Increase Mather and grandfather of Cotton Mather, was aboard the *James,* which had sailed out of Bristol, England, in late May 1635, bound for Boston.

Along with three other ships bound for the New World, the *James* and the *Angel Gabriel* had anchored at Milford Haven in Wales until a change in the wind enabled them to embark on June 22. The *James,* a merchant ship, and the larger, slower *Angel Gabriel* stayed close to each other for the first part of the transatlantic crossing, but they eventually parted ways so that the *James* could take advantage of a favorable wind.

The *James* ran into difficult weather off New England, and the two ships arrived at the coast at about the same time—the *James* at the Isles of Shoals and the *Angel Gabriel* farther north. The *James* had about a hundred passengers, including Richard Mather, his father, mother, and four brothers.

On August 13, as the *James* sailed down the coast toward Boston, it passed stark Boon Island a few miles off the coast of southern Maine. The crew intended to anchor for the night off Hog Island (now Appledore Island) in the Isles of Shoals, a craggy archipelago several miles off New Hampshire and the southernmost Maine coast.

According to Mather, "Ye wind being strong at south-southwest they could not atteyne ye purpose, and so were forced to lye off againe to sea all night." Slow progress was made the next day, and finally the crew was able to anchor at the Isles of Shoals. At daybreak the crew and passengers found themselves in a dire situation. Mather wrote in his journal:

> The Lord sent forth a most terrible storm of rain and easterly wind, whereby we were in as much danger as, I think, ever people were. For we lost in that morning three great anchors and cables; . . . two were broken by the violence of the waves, and the third cut by the seamen in extremity and distress, to save the ship and their and our lives. And when our cables and anchors were all lost, we had no outward means of deliverance but by loosing sail, if so be we might get to the sea from amongst the islands and rocks where we anchored. But the Lord let us see that our sails could not save us neither, no more than our cables and anchors. For, by the force of the wind and rain, the sails were rent in sunder and split in pieces, as if they had been but rotten rags.

The loss of the ship and its passengers appeared to be imminent, but a sudden and fortunate change in the wind enabled the *James* to escape the rocky ledges. Mather saw the escape as a direct answer to the terrified passengers' prayers:

> In this extremity and appearance of death, as distress and distraction would suffer us, we cried unto the Lord, and he was pleased to have compassion and pity upon us; for by his overruling providence and his own immediate good hand, he guided the ship past the rock, assuaged the violence of the sea and of the wind and rain, and gave us a little respite to fit the ship with other sails, and sent us a fresh gale of wind . . . by which we went on that day in our course south-west and by west towards Cape Ann. It was a day much to be remembered,

The seal of the Pemaquid settlement bore the image of the *Angel Gabriel*. The "A.E." on the seal referred to the initials of the patentees, and 1631 was the date of the patent.

because on that day the Lord granted us as wonderful a deliverance as, I think, ever people had, out of as apparent danger as I think ever people felt.

The *James* miraculously survived to reach Boston within a few days. Among the fortunate passengers was eleven-year-old Jonathan Mitchell, who went on to graduate from Harvard and to become an influential minister in Cambridge, Massachusetts.

Meanwhile, some seventy miles up the coast, those on board the *Angel Gabriel* were engaged in their own life-and-death struggle. The *Angel Gabriel* was a 240-ton galleon, built in 1615 as the *Starre*. Under the name *Jason,* the ship had been captained by John Pennington and carried twenty-five cannons as part of Sir Walter Raleigh's expedition to Guiana, South America, in 1617.

By 1619 the *Jason* was purchased by two English merchants and renamed *Angel Gabriel*. The ship carried various cargoes in the following years. In 1627 the *Angel Gabriel* achieved a measure of fame when the crew repelled three attacking Spanish ships off Calais, France. A ballad of the day sang the praises of the ship and its crew. It began with this verse:

Attend you and give ear awhile,
and you shall understand
Of a battle fought upon the seas,
by a ship of brave command;
The fight it was so famous,
that all men's hearts doth fill.
And made them cry, "To sea,
With the Angel Gabriel."

In 1635 the *Angel Gabriel* became one of many ships involved in the "Great Migration" of Puritans to the New World. Four years earlier, two Englishmen had received a patent for 1,200 acres around a trading settlement at Pemaquid, a point of land in midcoast Maine between Muscongus Bay and John Bay. The Pemaquid settlement was the *Angel Gabriel's* intended destination.

It isn't clear how many passengers were aboard the *Angel Gabriel* for its final voyage. Warren Riess's *Angel Gabriel: The Elusive English Galleon* informs us that an exhaustive search of archival records and family lore has revealed the names of twenty-five passengers. The captain is believed to have been Robert Andrews, a native of Norwich, England.

The ship carried sixteen guns. It's probable that it was also transporting a large amount of goods to the Pemaquid settlement, which would account for the relatively small number of passengers.

It's hard to get a clear picture of precisely what happened to the *Angel Gabriel* in the hurricane. Mather claimed that the ship was "burst to pieces and cast away in ye storme" while at anchor. Another contemporary chronicler, Edward Trelawny, wrote that the *Angel Gabriel* "was Caste away as she ridd att Anchor in Pemaquidd."

Thomas Vanburen Haines, whose ancestor Samuel Haines was on board the ship, wrote in 1902: "During the storm the wind changed from north-east to north-west. The *Angel Gabriel,* probably now feeling the full force of the wind, was torn from her anchorage, and dashed in pieces upon the shore."

The ship was a complete loss in any case, and the scene was undoubtedly one of confusion and chaos as the passengers and crew were swept ashore. Mather reported that one crewman and three or

The 1635 wreck of the *Angel Gabriel* occurred near Pemaquid Point, now the site of one of Maine's most popular lighthouses.
U.S. Coast Guard photo.

four passengers lost their lives; the precise number and identities of those who died are unknown. Most of the cargo was lost, along with most of the belongings of those aboard.

Among the passengers was John Cogswell (1587–1669), a wealthy London merchant, who was traveling with his wife and eight of their children. Cogswell had sold his mills and real estate holdings in England before embarking for America.

A legal battle involving descendants of John Cogswell developed in 1676. Samuel Haines, then sixty-five years old, had been aboard the *Angel Gabriel* as Cogswell's apprentice. In his testimony he stated that a number of the Cogswells' belongings had been saved from the wreck, including feather beds and other bedding, a large quantity of brass and pewter items, and a Turkish carpet.

William Furber, another apprentice or servant who was barely out of his teens at the time of the wreck of the *Angel Gabriel*, also testified in the 1676 case. Furber recalled that Cogswell had recovered

Ruby Lang, a diver, inspects an iron anchor during the search for the *Angel Gabriel*. The anchor was found to be of a later vintage (circa 1840–60) than the *Angel Gabriel*. Photo by Phil Voss, courtesy of the Darling Marine Center.

a tent along with other belongings from the ship, and that Cogswell lived for a time in the tent at the Pemaquid settlement. Soon after, Cogswell and his family relocated down the coast to Ipswich, Massachusetts.

Another of the *Angel Gabriel*'s survivors was John Bailey (1590–1651), a native of Chippenham, Wilts, England, who was a weaver by trade. Bailey was so thoroughly traumatized by his experience in the 1635 storm that he refused to brave the Atlantic for the rest of his life. Meanwhile, his wife in England, upon reading his description of the events, became too terrified to sail across the ocean to join her husband. Thus, the Baileys never saw each other again.

For years sport divers looked for the remains of the *Angel Gabriel,* with no success. Warren Riess was a graduate student in nautical archaeology at Texas A & M University in 1976 when he decided to search for the elusive remains of the ship. Discovery and excavation of the remains, Riess felt, could answer some important questions in nautical archaeology and maritime history. The supplies the ship was carrying could also reveal a great deal about the early settlement at Pemaquid.

Riess's search for the wreck and related research, aided by countless experts and volunteers, continued sporadically until 1996. At one point two young scallop divers told Riess that they had discovered lead ingots on the sea floor near Pemaquid Harbor. Riess believed the *Angel Gabriel* could have indeed carried such lead ingots as part of its cargo, but the tantalizing clue led nowhere; the young men had forgotten the exact location.

Riess, today a research associate professor of history and marine sciences at the University of Maine, never found any evidence of the *Angel Gabriel*'s final resting place. His years of work, however, revealed what an important role the vessel played in English and early American colonial history. Riess's labors also laid the groundwork for any future expedition searching for the elusive shipwreck.

In his 1891 volume, *Historic Storms of New England,* Sidney Perley relates a curious footnote to the 1635 hurricane. It seems there was an old man in Ipswich, Massachusetts, who often took his boat out to sea. The man's only companion on these voyages was his dog, who had learned to steer the boat. The pair was seen in the boat on the Ipswich River as the storm approached, headed for the ocean. The man was warned of the storm. Before continuing on his way, he declared, "I will go to sea, though the devil were there." The boat, dog, and man were never seen again.

CHAPTER TWO

The *Nottingham Galley* at Boon Island, 1710

TOURISTS on the southern Maine coast flock each summer to York's Sohier Park to ogle the Cape Neddick "Nubble" Lighthouse—slightly offshore, tidy, and pretty as a postcard. Those with sharp eyes or long lenses might notice, some seven miles distant, a dark, needlelike lighthouse rising like a mirage from a low-lying, grayish island on the horizon. This is Boon Island, or, as the celebrated New Hampshire seacoast author Celia Thaxter aptly described it, the "forlornest place that can be imagined."

The barren, rocky islet is about four hundred square yards in size, and only fourteen feet above sea level at its highest point. In the summer of 1682 a coastal trading vessel, the *Increase,* was wrecked on its ledges. The four survivors—three white men and one Indian—spent a month on the island, living on fish and gulls' eggs. One day the men saw smoke rising from Mount Agamenticus several miles away, so they built a fire in response. The Indians at Mount Agamenticus saw the smoke from the island, and the stranded men were soon rescued.

The precise origins of the island's name are shrouded in four centuries of history. It's been often stated that the men from the *Increase,* seeing their survival as a boon granted by God, were moved to name the island Boon. In fact, the island was referred to by that name long before the wreck of the *Increase.* John Winthrop mentioned it in his journal in 1630: "We saw, also, ahead of us, some four leagues from shore, a small rock, called Boone Isle, not above a flight shot over, which hath a dangerous shoal to the E. and by S. of it, some two leagues in length."

The island was also mentioned five years later in Richard Mather's journal; like Winthrop, he spelled it "Boone." Another early spelling of the island's name was "Bone," not inappropriate for a location where so many mariners met their doom.

According to some writers, including the popular New England historian Edward Rowe Snow, the island's name stemmed from the practice of local fishermen who left barrels of provisions on the island for the benefit of shipwrecked sailors. That would certainly have been a "boon" in such circumstances. Exactly when that tradition began and ended isn't clear, but it appears that nothing of the sort was going on in 1710.

The wreck of the *Nottingham Galley* was one of the most famous maritime episodes of the early eighteenth century, rivaling the story of the *Bounty* a few decades later for notoriety. The story has all the juicy drama one could ask for: a shipwreck in a blinding storm, a conflict between the captain and first mate, and men resorting to desperate measures to stay alive in the most extreme conditions imaginable.

John Deane, the man most closely identified with the 1710 wreck, was born in Nottingham in central England—a locale associated with the legend of Robin Hood—in 1679. After some experience as an apprentice butcher and drover, he became involved in the poaching of local livestock.

Deane escaped the consequences of his crimes by leaving to join the Royal Navy. According to an 1870 biographical novel by W. H. G. Kingston, *John Deane of Nottingham,* Deane had never set foot on a ship before he joined the Royal Navy when he was about seventeen.

Deane made such an impression in the siege of Gibraltar in 1704 that he was soon promoted to captain at the tender age of twenty-five. He bought his own ship in 1709 and named it the *Nottingham Galley,* after his birthplace. Deane's brother Jasper and several other men bought shares in the new enterprise. A local businessman named Charles Whitworth was one of the investors.

The *Nottingham Galley* was a small vessel of 120 tons, with ten

Barren Boon Island, scene of the wreck of the *Nottingham Galley,* is now home to New England's tallest lighthouse. Photo by Jeremy D'Entremont.

guns. In 1710 Deane had the ship loaded with a cargo of cordage that he intended to take to Boston. After taking on an additional cargo of butter and cheese in Ireland, the *Nottingham Galley* set sail for Boston on September 25, 1710, with fourteen men aboard. Among the crewmen was the captain's brother Henry and Miles Whitworth, the son of Charles Whitworth.

The southern Maine coast was first sighted in early December. As the crew tried to take the vessel south along the coast to Boston, a violent storm was encountered on December 11. Deane later wrote:

> Meeting with contrary winds and bad weather, it was the beginning of December when we first made land to the eastward of Piscataqua, and proceeding southward for the bay of Massachusetts, under a hard gale of wind at northeast, accompanied with rain, hail, and snow, having no observation for ten or twelve days, we, on the 11th, handed all our sails, excepting our fore-sail and maintop-sail double-reefed, ordering one hand forward to look out. Between eight and nine o'clock, going forward myself, I saw the breakers ahead, whereupon I called out to put the helm hard to starboard; but before the ship could wear we struck upon the east end of the rock called Boon-Island, four leagues to the eastward of Piscataqua.

The masts quickly snapped and fell. The sleet stung the men's faces, and the stormy night was black, but they somehow managed to clamber onto the island's slippery ledges. Deane, meanwhile, tried in vain to save some items from inside the ship, but it was too late: the stern was underwater by this time. In his words:

> I threw myself with all the strength I had toward the rock; but it being low water, and the rock extremely slippery, I could get no hold, and tore my fingers, hands, and arms in the most deplorable manner, every wash of the sea fetching me off again, so that it was with the utmost peril and difficulty that I got safe on shore at last. The rest of the men ran the same hazards, but, through the mercy of Providence, we all escaped with our lives.

The men crept about trying to find shelter from the wind, sleet, and snow, but there was none to be found. They endured a cold, terrifying night; the men had no way of knowing whether high tide would leave the island and its occupants completely submerged. Some wreckage from the ship was found at daybreak, but nothing edible was salvaged except a few small bits of cheese.

Since everything was thoroughly soaked, efforts to light a fire were useless. A makeshift tent was created using pieces of sail and canvas salvaged from the wreck. When night fell again, the men huddled together to keep from freezing. By noon on the second day the captain was informed that the ship's cook, who had been ill before the wreck, had died. "None mentioned eating him," Deane wrote, "though several, with myself, afterward acknowledged that they had thoughts of it."

By the third day, the men's hands and feet were numb to the point of being almost useless. At the captain's urging, they pulled off their shoes and found that the skin and nails came easily off their discolored feet. The men then wrapped their feet in canvas and oakum (tarred fiber picked from the ropes salvaged from the ship).

As their strength waned in the following days, the men improved the tent and placed a piece of cloth in the form of a flag on top of it, in the hope that it might catch the eye of a mariner on a passing vessel. The tent was so small that when all the men were inside, they had to lie back to back; there was not enough room for anyone to turn over unless all did it at the same time.

In the first week, the men survived on bits of cheese, seaweed, and some beef bones that were beaten into small pieces so that they could be swallowed.

A makeshift boat was constructed from timber and other wreckage from the *Nottingham Galley*. The ship's carpenter wasn't able to assist in the task; he had fallen so ill that he wasn't even able to offer advice. By December 21 the boat was declared seaworthy. It was decided that Captain Deane, being the strongest, would be the skipper of the little vessel in the attempt to reach the mainland.

Chosen to accompany Deane on the mission were his brother Henry, the first mate, Christopher Langman, and four others. As they tried to launch the boat into deep water, a large swell flipped the boat over and broke it to pieces, "totally disappointing our enterprize and destroying all our hopes at once," Deane wrote. The wind soon increased and the seas grew heavy. The men realized that even if they had successfully launched the boat, they most likely would have perished before reaching shore.

In his account of the ordeal, Deane described the condition of the survivors at this juncture:

> We were now reduc'd to the most deplorable and mallancholy Circumstance imaginable, almost every Man but myself, weak to an extremity, and near starved with Hunger and Cold; their Hands and Feet frozen and mortified, with large and deep ulcers in their legs (the very smell offensive to those of us, who could creep into the air) and nothing to dress them with, but a Piece of linnen that was cast on shoar. No Fire, and the weather extream cold; our small stock of Cheese spent, and nothing to support our feeble Bodies but Rock-weed and a few Muscles, scarce and difficult to get (at most, not above two or three for each man a day). So that we had our miserable bodies perishing, and our poor disconsolate spirits overpowered, with the deplorable Prospect of starving, without any appearance of relief.

There was some rekindling of hope when Langman was able to kill a seagull. Deane divided the meat equally among the men, "tho' raw and scarce every one a mouthful."

The men managed to cobble together another small raft, meant to carry two men to the mainland. One of the men chosen to make the attempt, an excellent swimmer, was referred to by Deane as "a Sweed." The men were instructed to light a fire when they reached shore as a signal to the men on Boon Island.

The raft was launched in high seas in the afternoon. No signal fire was seen, and Deane and the other survivors would later learn that the raft was found wrecked onshore two days later. One of the men was found, dead, with a paddle still fastened to his wrist. The "Sweed" was never seen again.

A green hide (a skin that wasn't completely dried or tanned) was found washed onto the island, and Deane minced it into small pieces so that the men could swallow it. This lucky find helped keep them alive, but the men were slowly starving to death.

As the calendar approached the end of the year and the men's stay on Boon Island surpassed two weeks, the ship's carpenter, a man of about forty-seven described by Deane as "a fat Man, and naturally of a dull, heavy, Phlegmatick Constitution and Disposition," died, having been incapacitated almost from the time of the wreck.

The men began to petition Deane with a shocking, yet easily understandable, plea: they wanted to eat the body of the carpenter. Deane knew there was no reasonable alternative. He later wrote:

> After abundance of mature thought and consultation about the lawfullness or sinfullness on the one Hand, and absolute Necessity on the other; Judgment, Conscience, &c. were oblig'd to submit to the more prevailing arguments of our craving appetites; so that at last we determined to satisfie our hunger and support our feeble Bodies with the Carkass in Possession: first ordering his skin, head, hands, Feet and bowels to be buried in the Sea, and the Body to be quarter'd for Conveniency of drying and carriage, to which I again receiv'd for Answer, that they were not all of them able, but entreated I wou d perform it

An early 1800s engraving depicting the wreck of the *Nottingham Galley* at Boon Island. From the collection of Edward Rowe Snow, courtesy of Dorothy Bicknell.

for them: A task very greivous, and not readily comply d with, but their incessant Prayers and Intreaties at last prevaild, and by night I had performed my labour.

Deane cut the flesh into thin slices, which he washed in salt water. The men ate seaweed with the flesh, "instead of bread." They ate so voraciously, "their eyes staring and looking wild," that Deane took the precaution of moving the rest of the carpenter's remains far from the tent, out of easy reach.

On January 2, after three weeks on the island, Deane emerged from the tent to catch sight of an approaching shallop. Upon discovering the wrecked raft on the mainland, some men had ventured out to look for shipwreck survivors. Because of heavy swells around the rocky shore of the island, the vessel had to anchor about a hundred yards away. A few hours later, as the seas subsided, one man was sent to make a difficult landing on the island in a canoe.

On seeing Deane and the others looking so "ghastly and frightful," the man in the canoe was "so affrighted" that he could barely respond to Deane's questions. He provided the shipwrecked men with materials to make a fire and then left, promising that a vessel would return the next day to take the men to Portsmouth.

With fire, the men were able to warm themselves and to broil their "meat." The next day was stormy and no vessel was seen, but on the day after that a shallop arrived from Portsmouth. The survivors were transferred to the shallop aboard a canoe, two or three at a time, and were fed rum and bread. They became violently ill, but just as quickly recovered, their appetites ravenous. The ten survivors recovered, although some lost the use of their limbs.

Before he returned to England, the first mate, Christopher Langman, filed a deposition before Samuel Penhallow, a justice of the peace in Portsmouth. Langman's statement, backed by two other crewmen from the *Nottingham Galley,* claimed that Captain Deane had tried to turn the ship over to privateers near England, and had then deliberately wrecked it so that he and the other investors could collect insurance money. Langman also claimed that Deane had physically assaulted him on the night of the shipwreck.

Soon after John Deane returned to England, his brother Jasper published the captain's own account of the *Nottingham Galley* disaster: *A Narrative of the Sufferings, Preservation, and Deliverance of Capt. John Deane and Company; In the Nottingham Galley of London, Cast Away on Boon Island, near New England, December 11, 1710.* Jasper Deane attested to his brother's truthfulness in the preface: "I presume any Person acquainted with my Brother will readily believe the Truth hereof."

Captain Deane cast himself in a positive light in his narrative, and nothing about the account suggests obvious fabrication or exaggeration. Within months, Christopher Langman's very different account was published, *A True Account of the Voyage of the Nottingham Galley of London, John Deane Commander, from the River Thames to New England.* Langman shared credit for the narrative with Nicholas Mellen, boatswain, and George White, sailor.

Langman began his account by asserting that four of the guns aboard the *Nottingham Galley* were useless, and that no more than six of the crewmen were suited to sailing in rough weather.

Before the ship arrived in Ireland to pick up goods there,

Langman wrote, the captain was overheard to say that he "would rather run the Ship ashore than perform his Voyage, if he thought he could be safe with the Insurers, because his Brother had insur'd 300£ upon her." Deane was plainly seen making preparations to ground the ship for financial gain, according to the account, and the voyage was saved by the efforts of Langman, who safely navigated the ship to Killybegs in Ireland.

Langman went so far as to accuse Captain Deane, along with his brother Henry, of attempted murder. Shortly before the wreck at Boon Island, according to Langman, Henry Deane repeatedly struck the mate in the head with a bottle of water, and John Deane followed by striking him with a periwig block (a wig stand).

Langman wrote that he was left for dead, but he soon recovered enough to warn the captain that he was sailing too close to the shore. Captain Deane's response, according to Langman, was to threaten to shoot the mate. A short time later the *Nottingham Galley* ran aground at Boon Island.

The wreck was deliberate, Langman claimed, but its severity was more than the captain had bargained for. Langman wrote that Deane told the men to prepare for death, as there could be no escape. "Then the Captain," Langman wrote, "who had been Cursing and Swearing before, began to cry and howl for Fear of losing his Life."

The Langman account continues in this vein: Deane is portrayed as a sniveling coward who knowingly endangered the lives of the crew and did nothing to save them. Langman asserted that Deane was the one who first proposed that the corpse of the carpenter be eaten, and that "there was no Man that eat more of the Corps than himself."

Langman concluded his version by giving his oath: "That this is the Truth; and that if the said Master had taken the Mate's Advice, the Ship, with God's Assistance, might have been in Boston Harbour several days before she was lost."

A third, apparently unauthorized version of the *Nottingham Galley* story appeared in print in London in 1711. This version sensationalized the cannibalism angle, claiming that the men cast lots to see who "would be the next Devor'd." Yet another abbreviated version appeared in Boston that year, a sermon on the wreck by Cotton Mather serving as its preface.

There's no doubt that John Deane's reputation was hurt by the publicity surrounding the wreck. Legend holds that Jasper Deane was so distressed by the whole episode that he died after suffering a ruptured blood vessel in a fight with his brother.

John Deane soon fled to Russia, where he accepted a commission as a lieutenant in the Russian Navy. This period of Deane's life is chronicled in two papers by Richard Warner: *Captain John Deane and the Wreck of the Nottingham Galley,* and *Deane: Mercenary, Diplomat, Spy.*

In 1714–15 Deane commanded the fifty-gun man-of-war *Yagudil* from Archangel, Russia, to Norway. Nearly half the crew perished in the difficult voyage. Deane's fortunes improved; he captured more than twenty ships in the next few years, during a long war with Sweden, and he built a reputation as a brave and daring commander.

In 1722 Deane was expelled from Russia along with many other mercenaries. Back in England, he wrote *A History of the Russian Fleet during the Reign of Peter the Great.* Deane promoted himself as an expert on the inner workings of Russian naval affairs, which led to a few years spent as a spy in St. Petersburg. Deane eventually became the commercial consul for the Ports of Flanders at Ostend, a post he held from 1728 until his retirement in 1738. He died in 1761.

The *Nottingham Galley* saga gained new notoriety when the historical novelist Kenneth Roberts published his book *Boon Island* in 1956. Roberts, a native of Kennebunk, Maine, had written a series of highly popular novels beginning in the 1920s, including *Arundel, The Lively Lady, Rabble in Arms, Northwest Passage,* and *Lydia Bailey. Boon Island,* his final novel, was not well received by critics on its initial release, but it was widely read and remains in print.

Roberts came down clearly on the side of Deane's version of events, but he included the disclaimer that the characters and incidents in the book were "entirely the product of the author's imagination." He chose to tell the story in the first person through the eyes of the crewman Miles Whitworth.

Aaron Taylor, an intern at the Darling Marine Center of the University of Maine, doing conservation work on one of the cannons from the *Nottingham Galley.* Photo by Linda Healy, courtesy of Darling Marine Center.

In his book *The Fury of the Seas,* the New England historian Edward Rowe Snow wrote that he visited Roberts around the time *Boon Island* was released. Roberts told Snow that he considered Langman's account a fraud, as he believed Deane never could have obtained his important post in Ostend if Langman's version was true. Snow wasn't so sure; he believed that graft and corruption could have accounted for Deane's appointment as consul at Ostend. As the tercentennial of the wreck of the *Nottingham Galley* approaches, we're no closer to knowing the whole truth about the wreck. Was Deane a hero or scoundrel? If Langman and his backers were lying, what was their motivation? Was Langman jealous, as Roberts suggested, of all the attention lavished on Deane? Was he simply a spiteful man?

It has proven easier to recover relics of the *Nottingham Galley* than to answer these questions. In 1995 nine small iron cannons and other artifacts (cannonballs, musket shot, and two grenades) believed to be from the *Nottingham Galley* were brought up from about twenty-five feet of water near Boon Island. Urchin divers had first spotted the cannons about fifteen years earlier.

Warren Riess, a nautical archaeologist, headed the recovery operation. After five years of conservation treatment at the University of Maine, the nine cannons are in the collection of the Maine State Museum in Augusta.

Chapter Three

The Doomed Penobscot Expedition
of 1779

THE PENOBSCOT EXPEDITION, the largest naval expedition of the American Revolution, has been called our nation's worst naval disaster until Pearl Harbor. It was a humiliating blow to the American cause, but its aftermath yielded a tantalizing treasure trove for shipwreck researchers. The ongoing study of the remains of the approximately thirty vessels that sank as a result of the expedition is likely to continue for years to come.

On June 12, 1779, a small fleet of British vessels, commanded by Brigadier General Francis McLean, arrived in Maine's Bagaduce (or Majabagaduce) River, near Penobscot Bay. The convoy, which had left Halifax, Nova Scotia, about two weeks earlier, carried almost seven hundred troops.

A few days later some of the men went ashore on the Bagaduce Peninsula (now the Castine Peninsula), between the entrances to the Bagaduce and Penobscot rivers, and began to construct fortifications on a bluff some two hundred feet above the sea. The site of the fort was near Dice (or Dyce) Head, now home to a photogenic lighthouse.

The fort, called Fort George, was intended to be part of a new British province to be called New Ireland, encompassing a large area between the Penobscot River and the St. Croix River. The fort also served to protect British shipping in the vicinity, and it was intended to be a refuge for American loyalists fleeing the colonies. The alarmed local populace was assured by General McLean that if they "would mind their business, and be peaceable," the inhabitants would not be disturbed.

Some families fled, but many others went to the new settlement to sign an oath of loyalty to King George III. They found the promise of money and trade with the British a welcome alternative to the earlier blockade of the coast that had stymied business. General McLean reported that the "misery of the people" in the vicinity was "hardly to be express'd."

Maine was part of Massachusetts at the time, and word of the British occupation of the Bagaduce Peninsula reached Boston by June 23. A committee of the legislature met hastily to consider a course of action. On the next day the committee recommended that the Board of War gather every armed vessel in Massachusetts that could be ready to sail within six days.

On July 1 Brigadier General Solomon Lovell of the militia was put in charge of the land forces being readied to sail to Maine. Until then Lovell's most notable experience as a commander was in an unsuccessful campaign to drive the British from Rhode Island in 1778. He had also taken part in the capture of Dorchester Heights in March 1776.

Captain Dudley Saltonstall was put in command of the fleet for the expedition. Saltonstall had earned a reputation over many years as a skilled commander, and he was the senior of five captains named when Congress created a navy in 1775.

The men who took command of the vessels in the expedition were mostly privateers, and they were probably threatened or bribed to go along. Among the other officers chosen for the expedition was Lieutenant Colonel Paul Revere, who was put in charge of the artillery.

Confidence was high as an impressive roster of ships gathered in Boston, Newburyport, and other ports in preparation for the Penobscot Expedition. So confident were the organizers that General George Washington, commander in chief of the Continental Army, was not even informed of the operation.

All told, the expedition consisted of about forty vessels, on board which were about 800 marines, 100 artillerymen, and some 1,200 militiamen. The militia consisted largely of boys and old men. The fleet included three Continental Navy vessels, three Massachusetts vessels, one New Hampshire vessel, and nine privateering ships, mounting a total of about 350 guns. The largest vessel was the thirty-two-gun ship *Warren* of the Continental Navy. There were also approximately twenty transport vessels.

The numbers were impressive, but the two commanders failed to come up with a common strategy, and the militia was hastily assembled and ill equipped. It's also generally believed that the ship captains were reluctant to take orders from Saltonstall.

On July 24, while Lovell was anchored near the Fox Islands in Penobscot Bay, some Penobscot Indians came aboard and offered to join the expedition. The British had tried to enlist the Indians in their cause, but they had refused. Lovell accepted their offer to help.

The next day Captain Philip Brown was sent to scout the situation at the Bagaduce Peninsula. The British flag flew over Fort George; three smaller batteries and three anchored sloops of war guarded the entrance to the harbor. On the way back to the *Warren,* Brown picked up three sympathizers at the small British battery on Banks Island (now Nautilus Island). The sympathizers informed Saltonstall that the fort on the peninsula was far from finished. Brown urged Saltonstall to attack immediately.

Saltonstall, who was familiar with the treacherous tides and currents in Penobscot Bay, waited until the wind and tide were favorable and moved the fleet close to the Bagaduce Peninsula by late afternoon. Some of the ships were ordered to attack and run out again, in an attempt to move the British sloops from their defensive positions. The American vessels were met with return fire from the British sloops and shore batteries. The cannonading continued into the evening, though little damage was sustained by either side.

Meanwhile, General Lovell's troops began to go ashore in boats, landing on a beach on the peninsula. As the boats arrived at the beach, they were met by an enemy ambush, and one of the Indians was killed. Lovell's men hastily retreated in their boats. Another attempt to land was made at daybreak on the next day, July 26, but again the attempt was repulsed.

Later that morning, Captain John Brewer, who had been inside Fort George two days before, recommended that the Patriots attack the defenses head-on, landing under the cover of their own guns. He believed that the fort could be taken in a half hour. Saltonstall replied that he would not risk his ships "in that damned hole."

Late that day the Americans finally gained some ground when a contingent of marines took the battery on Banks Island. The men set about building a breastwork on the island, and Revere sent more men and cannons. The position was greatly strengthened by dawn on July 27. At nine o'clock in the morning the men on the island began firing on the British ships. The shots did some damage and wounded a few of the British aboard the sloop-of-war *Albany*.

A council of war was held aboard the *Warren* on July 27, and it was decided that more than 1,100 troops would land at Bagaduce Bluff at midnight. The men couldn't all land at once, so the assault began in dense fog over the course of several hours, under cover of the American ships' guns.

There were losses on both sides, but the Americans gained significant ground and took a small battery in the assault. Lovell wrote,

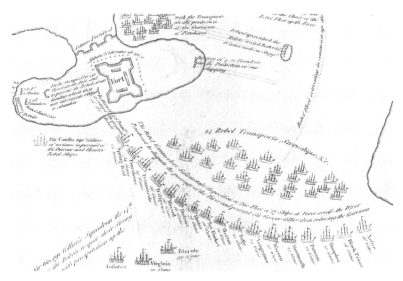

Detail from a 1785 map showing the American ships near the Castine Peninsula during the Penobscot Expedition. Boston Public Library.

"When I returned to the Shore, it struck me with admiration to see what a Precipice we had ascended. . . . it is at least where we landed three hundred feet high, and almost perpendicular, & the men were obliged to pull themselves by the twigs & trees."

Lovell was urged by Paul Revere to storm the fort, but he ordered a halt instead, believing the best strategy was to dig in for a siege. Lovell had his troops build a battery within a quarter mile of Fort George. Meanwhile, a messenger went by whaleboat to Machias, requesting more troops. Another messenger took a dispatch describing the situation to Boston.

During the day on July 28 the American ships under Saltonstall's command bombarded the British sloops. The masts and rigging of the *Warren* were damaged by return fire, and Saltonstall ordered his crew to retreat. That night the British naval commander, Captain Henry Mowat, moved his ships deeper into the harbor, out of reach of American cannons.

At the fort General McLean was operating under the belief that the American forces were much larger than they actually were, a conclusion that was based on the number of ships. McLean believed that the only way the British might be able to hold on to the fort was to wait for reinforcements. He ordered small groups of fifers and drummers to march near the enemy positions in an effort to keep them off guard.

On July 29 a dispatch was received from the Navy Board, urging Saltonstall and Lovell to push on "with Vigour, Conceiving no time is to be lost" before British reinforcements could arrive. In spite of this, Saltonstall and Lovell continued to exercise the utmost caution.

A new assault on one of the British batteries was staged by the Americans in the predawn hours of August 1; marines, militia, and sailors all took part. The British retreated to the fort, but at daybreak they were able to fire the fort's guns at the Americans. The attackers were forced to retreat to their line, relinquishing the battery.

The standoff continued. George E. Buker, in his comprehensive book *The Penobscot Expedition,* points out that the American and British commanders were both operating under false assumptions. McLean believed the rebel force was much larger than it was, and his conservative strategy consisted of cannonading and limited probing with light infantry. Lovell, believing his force was too small, feared an attack from the British. He dug in and continued with occasional skirmishes and cannonading, believing that naval support was needed to take the fort.

Captain Mowat, with only three sloops-of-war and their total of fifty guns, held off the much larger American force, as Saltonstall feared that his fleet would be unable to maneuver fast enough if it entered the harbor. As Buker pointed out in his book, much of Saltonstall's reluctance was related to the poor maneuverability of his square-rigged ships. Just the same, Lovell and the other officers in the expedition believed that the vastly superior American firepower would win the day if Saltonstall would only agree to attack. It would have been, after all, more than three hundred guns against fifty.

On August 5 Lovell informed Saltonstall of his opinion that no further progress was possible without substantial naval support. Saltonstall consulted with his ship captains, who almost unanimously agreed that they would attack only if Lovell's forces stormed the fort at the same time. Lovell's officers voted unanimously against this plan. A dispatch describing the situation was sent to Boston.

Saltonstall and five of his captains were reconnoitering in two or three small, unarmed boats on August 7 when they were discovered by the enemy. Eight British boats soon pursued the Americans, who beached their boats and ran into the woods. The officers, except Saltonstall, were soon rescued. The following morning Saltonstall, who had run so deep into the woods that he had become lost, was picked up on the shore and returned to his ship.

The standoff continued, with occasional skirmishes, as Lovell and Saltonstall awaited word from Boston. By August 12 local inhabitants became aware of the ominous sight of approaching ships in the fog. A squadron of British ships was gathering at Monhegan Island, including the formidable sixty-four-gun *Raisonable* and several heavily armed frigates. The fleet had left New York on August 3 under the command of Commodore Sir George Collier.

The deeply divided American commanders finally, on August

Dice Head Lighthouse in Castine stands today at the scene of
some of the fighting during the Penobscot Expedition in 1779.
Photo by Jeremy D'Entremont.

13, agreed on a plan of attack. Lovell took four hundred men to the
rear of the fort, and Saltonstall prepared to take five ships into the
harbor. Late that night Saltonstall received word of the British reinforcements. The Americans' belated attack was abandoned just as it
was beginning, and the retreat began.

Saltonstall at first hoped to fight off the advancing British ships
while the American transport vessels took most of the men to safety.
But as the first British ship drew within firing range, Saltonstall
announced that it was every man for himself. When the American
captains and crews saw the advancing fleet, they quickly scattered.

For the next two days the American fleet retreated up the Penobscot River under fierce pursuit by the British. Saltonstall hurried the
Warren past the transport ships, leaving them unprotected. Crews
abandoned their vessels, and many of the men spent several days in
the woods with little food.

Some of the ships were set on fire before being abandoned. The
Warren made it up the river as far as Oak Point Cove in Frankfort,

where it was burned. On August 16 the river near Bangor was littered with the smoldering hulks of the American vessels.

In his journal Lovell described the ignominious events: "To attempt to give a description of this terrible day is out of my power. It would be a fit subject for some masterly hand to describe it in its true colors;—to see four ships pursuing seventeen sail of armed vessels, nine of which were stout ships—transports on fire—men of war blowing up—provisions of all kinds, and every kind of stores on shore (at least in small quantities) throwing about, and as much confusion as can possibly be conceived."

Accounts vary, but about thirty American ships were destroyed by their own crews, and nine transport ships were captured. About five hundred Americans were killed or captured, and the Penobscot Expedition cost the Revolutionary cause the considerable sum of $7 million.

British sailors and marines salvaged what they could from the American vessels. An estimated fifty or sixty cannons were saved by the British, and some of them were installed at Fort George. Some were taken to an armory at Halifax, Nova Scotia. Other materials from the ships were salvaged over the years by local inhabitants.

A Massachusetts court of inquiry found that the primary reason for the defeat was the "want of proper spirit and energy in the commander." Saltonstall was court-martialed aboard a frigate in Boston Harbor and subsequently dismissed from the navy. Revere was also relieved of his command, but he was ultimately cleared of all charges.

The British held Bagaduce until the end of the war. In July 1780 an American detachment achieved some measure of revenge when it sailed near Fort George and took two British sloops that were carrying American cannons taken in the failed expedition. Forty British prisoners were secured along with the sloops. According to a newspaper account, the Americans "fired at the fort to vex the enemy and got safe away."

One of the interesting footnotes of the Penobscot Expedition concerns a trunk packed with the creations of Paul Revere. The master silversmith, who was in charge of the expedition's artillery,

The deteriorating upper edge of the wooden hull of the *Defence*, in muddy water near Stockton Springs. Courtesy of Warren Riess and the Darling Marine Center.

had hoped to sell the goods to other officers. After Revere had disembarked the *Spring Bird* as it retreated, the captain had the vessel burned as the British closed in. The *Spring Bird* was seen to sink with Revere's trunk aboard. Try as they might, no divers have been able to recover any of this treasure, or at least none has reported such a find.

The British sloop *Albany,* after its involvement in the Penobscot Expedition, was being used as a prison ship when it grounded and broke apart in Penobscot Bay on December 28, 1782.

Sunken reminders of the Penobscot Expedition have surfaced now and then over the years. Dredging operations around Bangor in the 1870s yielded several cannons. In 1953 workers building the Joshua Chamberlain Bridge between Bangor and Brewer found four iron cannons. Another brass cannon, forged at Paul Revere's shop, was recovered from the river at Brewer.

John Cayford, a welder involved in the bridge construction, later claimed to have located the remains of the *Warren* and the British transport vessel HMS *Providence*. A bronze six-pound cannon recovered by Cayford is on display at the Penobscot Marine Museum in Searsport.

One of the most exciting finds related to the expedition took place in 1972, when students and faculty from the Massachusetts Institute of Technology and the Maine Maritime Academy located the remains of the *Defence,* a 170-ton American brig that was sunk by its crew during the retreat. The *Defence* was built in Beverly, Massachusetts, just before the expedition got under way.

The wreck was found off the northeast corner of Sears Island near Stockton Springs, in about twenty-five feet of water. The team, led by W. F. Searle, used an experimental side-scan sonar unit developed at the Maine Maritime Academy. Excavation of the *Defence* showed that the crew had abandoned all their supplies, including food stores and personal items. A shot locker was found still full of cannonballs.

Surprisingly, 40 percent of the ship's hull was still intact, revealing much detail of the ship's design and construction. The officers' quarters, where the charge was set that destroyed the ship, was blown to bits.

Two cannons and other artifacts were salvaged from the site in 1973–74. Plymouth State College's Professor David Switzer led systematic excavations between 1975 and 1980, and hundreds of artifacts were recovered and sent to the Maine State Museum. The finds included a copper caboose (deck stove), a copper cauldron, pewter spoons, tools, navigational instruments, cannonballs, and buttons.

Between 1994 and 1997 University of Maine researchers located several submerged sites of interest. Warren Riess, Research Associate Professor of History and Marine Sciences, and his colleagues tentatively identified the remains of the *Warren,* as well as three other vessels.

From 1999 to 2001 the U.S. Naval Historical Center's (NHC) Underwater Archaeology Branch surveyed the Penobscot River as part of an ongoing effort to research shipwrecks associated with the Penobscot Expedition, in cooperation with the University of Maine and the Maine Historic Preservation Commission.

The focus of the NHC investigation was the "Phinney Site,"

believed to be the remains of one of the scuttled American ships, possibly the brig *Diligent*. The Phinney Site, in shallow water just off the eastern shore of the Penobscot River near the town of Brewer, was named for Brent Phinney, a Brewer resident who discovered it in 1998.

The artifacts found at the Phinney Site include a junior officer's brass shoe buckle, tobacco pipes, a four-inch folding pocketknife, hundreds of pieces of ceramic, glass, brick, and other materials, many cannonballs, and bar shot. James Hunter, an underwater archaeologist with the U.S. Navy, explained: "When fired from a cannon, bar shot would leave the bore and spin through the air, taking out rigging, sails, and people. They were grisly weapons."

A second nearby location, dubbed the "Shoreline Site," across the river near downtown Bangor, contained scattered Revolutionary-era cannons and shot. All in all, the disaster of 1779 has provided endless fodder for Maine history buffs and wreck researchers. As James Hunter has said, "Not everyone in the country is lucky enough to have a collection of historically significant shipwrecks right in their own back yard."

A multimedia exhibit on the Penobscot Expedition—the largest ever created on the subject—can be seen at the Castine Historical Society's museum in the former Abbott School on the Castine town common.

CHAPTER FOUR

The Circus Ship *Royal Tar*
in Penobscot Bay, 1836

WILLIAM IV, king of the United Kingdom of Great Britain and Ireland from 1830 to 1837, served in the Royal Navy as a young man and achieved the rank of rear admiral. This service earned him the nickname "Sailor King." He was, famously, also called "Silly Billy" for his rambling speeches. Another of William's nautical nicknames, "Royal Tar" ("tar," or "jack tar," is an old expression for sailor), was applied to several ships.

The *Royal Tar* that concerns us here was a 164-foot, 400-ton, wooden side-wheel steamship built at Saint John, New Brunswick, Canada, in 1836. The steamer made a local trial run on May 2 of that year. According to an article in the *New Brunswick Magazine,* there was "general jollification" on the initial voyage, and a hot luncheon was served along with "rivers of sherry and oceans of champagne." A toast was made to "the patriotic and beloved sovereign" for whom the ship was named.

On June 5 the *Royal Tar* made its first run to St. Andrews and Eastport, Maine, and the return trip was completed in a record-breaking five hours. The steamer also began making weekly runs to Portland, Maine.

On Friday, October 21, 1836, the *Royal Tar* left Peter's Wharf in Saint John, headed for Portland. The steamer must have resembled Noah's Ark: its unusual cargo included an elephant named Mogul, a Bengal tiger, two lions, two camels, six Arabian horses, monkeys, and many other exotic animals. The menagerie was part of a traveling circus known as Dexter's Locomotive Museum and Burgess' Collection of Serpents and Birds.

According to the 1841 book *The Tragedy of the Seas,* written by Charles Ellms, Mogul had achieved celebrity status. "His performances in the ring would scarcely be credited, had they not been daily witnessed by hundreds," Ellms wrote. "A word or a look was sufficient to stimulate him to the greatest exertions. He caressed his master in the best manner, and would not so readily obey another person. He received his orders with attention, and executed them cheerfully."

Also on board as part of the circus was a brass band, a large collection of waxworks, and an enormous two-ton show wagon—called an omnibus—along with several other wagons and accompanying horses. To make room for all this, two lifeboats were removed from the deck and left in Saint John.

Before boarding the steamship, the circus had been touring Nova Scotia and New Brunswick. "Everybody went to see the show, which was a great one for those times," wrote W. O. Raymond in the *New Brunswick Magazine.*

In charge of the *Royal Tar* was Captain Thomas Reed, with a crew of twenty-one and seventy-two passengers. Old sailors held many superstitions. Some believed that taking birds, snakes, or a brass band on a voyage would bring bad luck, and to leave on a Friday would surely tempt the fates. Reed believed none of that.

The weather was fair as the steamer cruised south, but around sunset a strong westerly wind sprung up, prompting Captain Reed to seek refuge in the harbor at Eastport. The *Royal Tar* left Eastport at two o'clock on Tuesday afternoon, but strong winds forced the steamship to take shelter at least two more times.

The voyage resumed from Machias Bay on the morning of Tuesday, October 25. At one-thirty that afternoon, as the steamer was about two miles off the Fox Islands Thoroughfare near Vinalhaven, it was discovered that the water had been allowed to go too low in the boiler. The pilot's son discovered the problem and told his father, who informed the second engineer.

The second engineer, a man named Marshall, at first insisted

A nineteenth-century engraving of the wreck of the *Royal Tar*. From the collection of Edward Rowe Snow, courtesy of Dorothy Bicknell.

that everything was fine. The first engineer, meanwhile, was asleep after working all night. Marshall had entrusted the ship's fireman to fill the boilers. According to some accounts, the steamer's regular engineer had recently been dismissed for economic reasons, so less experienced men were in charge.

The engine was stopped on the captain's orders and a safety valve was opened. Water was supplied to the boiler and all appeared to be well, until, about a half hour later, the vessel was found to be on fire below the deck, above the boiler.

The situation grew desperate just as the passengers were about to sit down for dinner. Captain Reed later described the situation: "The cable was slipped instantly and the fire engine set to work, but in five minutes the men could not stand at the pump, which was below, the smoke nearly suffocating them." A cabin boy appeared on deck, shouting, "Fire!"

Reed ordered the crew to fly a distress signal. The two lifeboats having been left behind in Saint John, the only boats available for escape were the longboat and the jolly boat. In the panic that ensued, the first engineer and fifteen other men jumped into the longboat and hastily rowed away, abandoning the women and children on the flaming steamer. The men made it safely to Isle au Haut, about seven miles away.

Captain Reed and two other men commandeered the jolly boat, which was a dinghy normally used to ferry people to or from the ship. A passenger, Hinson Patten, later wrote: "Capt. Reed took charge of the stern boat, with two men, and kept her off the steamboat, which was a very fortunate circumstance, as it was the means of saving from forty to fifty persons, and to him all credit is due for his deliberate and manly perseverance throughout the whole calamity."

The middle of the ship was in flames, and the passengers ran about at the bow and stern. One of them, William Marjoram, later said that he saw a lion in a cage on deck and thought of Psalm 57:4: "My soul is among lions. I lie even among those that are set on fire." Some of the animals were rushing around on the deck.

Six horses and the two camels were seen to go overboard. Mogul, the elephant, had been chained on deck. He found his way to a part of the ship that was not on fire, and he put his forefeet on the deck rail. He remained in that position for some two hours, confusion all around him.

Scenes of desperation were playing out all over the ship. One man secured a stocking holding a large number of silver dollars to his waist and then lowered himself over the side. When he let go of the rope, he sank immediately because of the great weight of the silver.

Another passenger, H. H. Fuller, who had been ill in his berth, emerged to witness a scene of utter chaos. The screams and noise "baffled description," he later wrote. When Fuller's coat caught fire, he managed to secure a rope, fastened to a tiller chain, around him. He dropped over the side of the steamer into the ocean, near about fifteen others who were hanging in a similar fashion.

As the waves washed over him, Fuller was able to support the additional weight of three men and a woman. He watched as another woman held desperately to the foot of the pilot, who was hanging from the side of the vessel nearby. When her arms gave out, the pilot was able to grab onto the woman's head with his feet.

The pilot held the woman that way for five minutes, until the seas washed her away from him. She was swept near an Irish immigrant, also hanging from a rope, and she clung to him until Reed and the others on the jolly boat were able to pull her aboard with the Irishman, Fuller, and the others attached to Fuller.

Another act of heroism was attributed to a passenger from Portland by the name of Waite, who was hanging on for his life alongside the steamer while at the same time grasping a trunk that contained $5,000. A desperate woman, struggling to stay above the waves, floated near him. Waite let go of his trunk, which disappeared beneath the waves, in order to save the woman.

The U.S. revenue cutter *Veto,* which had been stationed at Castine, soon approached the scene. The cutter's pilot was sent ahead in a rowboat. As he came close to the flames and heard the pleas of those aboard, the pilot reportedly panicked and returned to the *Veto.*

By most accounts, Captain Howland T. Dyer of the *Veto* performed heroically, despite some initial hesitation because he feared the elephant would jump onto his vessel. Dyer brought the *Veto* very close to the burning steamship, although the *Veto* had gunpowder aboard—so close that the schooner twice caught fire.

Some of the passengers hastily constructed and launched a makeshift raft. As they tried to make their escape, Mogul finally decided it was time to flee the ship. The huge animal smashed through the rail and jumped overboard, carrying with him some of the passengers who had been clinging to the rail. According to some accounts, he crashed onto the raft, killing some of its passengers.

A few days after the wreck, it was reported that some men aboard a schooner spotted the remains of the dead elephant floating out to sea. Some versions of the story describe the elephant swimming to an island, where he "quietly installed himself in a barn."

According to Captain Reed, Dyer rescued forty people from the *Royal Tar,* "who must have perished, had not the cutter come to our aid." Dyer was seriously wounded and burned during the ordeal.

This illustration of the *Royal Tar* disaster appeared in the 1841 book *The Tragedy of the Seas* by Charles Ellms.

In his official report on the disaster, Captain Ezekiel Jones of the revenue cutter *Morris* said that he had talked to many of the survivors about Captain Dyer, and that "they all look upon him as their preserver."

After being removed safely to the *Veto*, William Marjoram left the relative safety of that vessel to take people from the *Royal Tar* into the jolly boat to be transferred to the *Veto*. He saw a woman holding on to the bowsprit, her clothes burned off, a child in her arms. Unable to hold on any longer, the woman dropped into the sea. She was rescued, but her child drowned.

A male passenger and the first mate clung to the wreck for three hours before they were finally rescued. The last of the survivors were put aboard the *Veto* by five-thirty that afternoon, and the revenue cutter arrived at Isle au Haut at seven o'clock. The flaming hulk of the *Royal Tar*, completely engulfed in fire, drifted for miles before it disappeared from sight later that night, twenty miles from where it had caught fire.

It's believed that thirty-two people perished in the disaster. Only one elderly woman, who never made it to the deck, burned to death; the rest drowned. There was no insurance on the vessel, and the loss was thought to exceed $100,000.

On October 26 Captain Reed wrote to the steamboat agent in Portland: "I have no blame to attach to anyone—I think that it was pure accident. I am very stiffened from overexertion, but hope to be better shortly. The people here have been very kind indeed, and we are as well off as can be expected."

In a cruel twist of fate, Reed arrived home in Saint John to receive the news that his eighteen-year-old son had died. He had been in perfect health when his father left the harbor, but he had succumbed to a forty-eight-hour illness. He was buried a few hours after his father's return.

Reed was at first criticized by some, as might be expected, but he was eventually showered with praise for his admirable behavior in the disaster. The people of Saint John presented the captain with about $700 they had collected in recognition of his heroism. A steward, W. G. Brown, was given $110 in appreciation for his role in the rescues.

Reed went on to become harbormaster in Saint John in 1841; he was said to be a familiar and beloved figure on the city's waterfront, walking among the wharves with his faithful dog. He died in 1860.

According to the New England historian Edward Rowe Snow in his book *True Tales of Terrible Shipwrecks,* Reed often told people over the years about a great treasure chest, stuffed with gold and silver, that went to the bottom with the *Royal Tar.* Many fortune seekers have hunted for the wreck, with no success.

Snow wrote that his cousin Willis Snow, who was keeper for a time at Goose Rocks Lighthouse, in the Fox Islands Thoroughfare near North Haven, made several trips in an effort to find the wreck. He was able to spot cannons believed to be from the British man-of-war *Albany,* but never found a trace of the *Royal Tar.*

After his revenue cutter experience, Howland Dyer became the keeper at Brown's Head Lighthouse on Vinalhaven, serving from 1843 to 1864. He died in 1870.

A steamship named *Gazelle* succeeded the *Royal Tar.* It ran aground near Saint John in 1838, but there was no loss of life. The large, elegant new steamship *North America* replaced the *Gazelle* in 1839. A newspaper article in 1840 pointed out that the *North*

Dorothy Bicknell, daughter of the popular New England historian Edward Rowe Snow, holds a bone said to be from the foot of the elephant Mogul, who died in the *Royal Tar* disaster. The bone was in the collection of the writer Alton Hall Black-ington. From the collection of Edward Rowe Snow, courtesy of Dorothy Bicknell.

America's engines and boilers were so constructed "as to make it next to impossible to take fire."

A spectacular, two-hundred-square-foot animated diorama depicting the wreck of the *Royal Tar* enjoyed great success at the Union Hall in Portland in late 1836. A rhyme concocted after the disaster enjoyed some popularity, in spite of its lighthearted treatment of such a sad event:

> The *Royal Tar*, she went too far,
> Her boiler got too hot;
> She'll never see St. John again,
> Because she's gone to pot.

Many years later, the poet Wilbert Snow imagined the *Royal Tar* as a reappearing ghost ship in *Fate of the Royal Tar*. Here is an excerpt:

> They remembered and believed, for many a year
> On that autumn night a crowd would appear
> Looking out toward Eggemoggin Reach to behold
> The *Royal Tar* rising in a circle of gold.
> And some saw a sign that the flood of Noah's warning
> Would yield to fire on the Judgment Morning.
> But other folks went to bask in the glow
> Of the one great horror they would ever know.

CHAPTER FIVE

The Steamer *Bohemian* at Cape Elizabeth, 1864

T HE STEAMER *Bohemian* of the Montreal Ocean Steamship Company (also known as the Allan Line) was a three-masted iron vessel, bark-rigged, of 2,200 tons burden, valued at about $350,000. The *Bohemian* made regular summer runs between Liverpool, England, and Quebec, Canada, and winter runs between Liverpool and Portland, Maine. Portland was then considered a winter port for Canada.

Built five years earlier by W. Denny & Brothers of Dumbarton, Scotland, the *Bohemian* departed Liverpool on February 4, 1864, bound for Portland with 219 passengers—200 predominantly Irish immigrants in steerage and 19 cabin-class passengers—and a crew of 99 men.

The *Bohemian* was never a fast vessel by anyone's estimation, and this was a particularly slow transatlantic voyage through storms and rough seas. An infant died during the crossing. A cargo of silks and other goods was on board, valued at around $1 million.

On February 22 it appeared that the tedious voyage was coming to an end, as the *Bohemian* made its way along Cape Elizabeth toward Portland's harbor. Captain Richard Borland had been making transatlantic runs for the Montreal Company for eight years, and he was intimately familiar with the waters near Portland.

It was a hazy evening. A little after seven o'clock a lookout informed the captain that he could see two lights onshore—one fixed and one flashing. Borland knew that the lights were the Cape

Elizabeth Light Station, known locally as Two Lights. The unusual atmospheric conditions, however, tricked Borland into believing he was much farther offshore than was actually the case.

Borland thought he was five or six miles from shore. In reality, the *Bohemian* was only about two miles off Cape Elizabeth. Three lookouts were on duty, and the steamer was moving very slowly, only about two knots. Borland realized a pilot's help was needed, so he ordered distress rockets fired to attract the attention of a local pilot. The flares were sent up for about a half hour.

The captain was below deck checking his charts when a buoy was sighted close ahead, which prompted the first officer to order the engines stopped. The steamer slowly drifted forward. At about eight o'clock, there was a light shudder, and then a more pronounced one.

The 295-foot ship had struck Alden's Rock, a menacing obstruction in shallow water about two miles southeast of Cape Elizabeth Light Station. The ledge had been, until recently, marked with a bell on a small iron boat. The boat and bell had been removed in 1860, replaced by a silent buoy.

The jagged ledge ripped a hole in the engine room, and the engineer reported to the captain that the injury was severe. The captain ordered full steam, as he intended to beach the *Bohemian* on the mainland shore. Within about ten minutes, the rising waters stopped the engines.

Borland ordered the steamer's two guns fired. The starboard gun was fired, but the port gun was underwater before it could be readied. A few miles away, about a mile southeast of Portland Head Lighthouse, two men in a pilot boat, Benjamin Willard and Henry Miller, heard the single blast from the *Bohemian*. "We listened a long time," Willard wrote later, "but heard no other, and made up our minds that they were celebrating on board some vessel, as it was Washington's Birthday."

Borland ordered the *Bohemian*'s six lifeboats readied as the steamer began to sink. The *Bohemian* crept along for another two miles or so, to a position barely a half mile north of the two lighthouses at the Cape Elizabeth station. The captain ordered the two anchors dropped.

The *Bohemian* sank offshore from the Cape Elizabeth Light Station. The original two lighthouses at the station were replaced by cast-iron towers in 1874. The east light, seen here, remains an active aid to navigation. Photo by Jeremy D'Entremont.

Three of the lifeboats were designed to hold about a hundred people each, and the others were intended to hold about forty. One officer was designated to be in charge of each of the six boats. The passengers rushed onto the deck in great confusion. The first lifeboat was smoothly launched with eighty on board. As the second boat was being lowered, a pin broke. One end of the boat fell precipitously, violently heaving many passengers into the freezing ocean waves.

Accounts vary, but it appears that sixteen people died in the accident with the second lifeboat. When the boat eventually drifted ashore on its own, found with it were a dead man and child. All the casualties in the incident were Irish steerage passengers, including several women and children.

All the other lifeboats and their occupants made it safely to shore. Some of the boats weren't full when they were launched, but the men in the boats refused to go near the steamer to pick up others.

The wreck of the *Bohemian* is depicted in this mural, *Shipwreck at Night*, painted by Alzira Peirce. The work is on public display at the South Portland post office.

As the last boats were launched, some passengers jumped into the water and attempted to climb into them. One who jumped was a woman who had lashed her infant to her shoulders. The woman and baby were rescued, but many others who jumped drowned.

The captain, the boatswain, three other crewmen, and seventy or eighty passengers were left stranded as the steamer continued to sink. About fifty women and children climbed into the foretop, a platform at the top of the foremast, out of reach of the rising waters. The remaining men climbed into the rigging.

The steamer continued to sink until around ten-thirty that night, when it settled in four or five fathoms of water, only about an eighth of a mile from shore. The deck was barely above the water at low tide. Those who were unable or unwilling to climb out of harm's way were swept off into the sea.

A few of the lifeboats returned before midnight and the rest of the passengers were safely removed. Borland and some of the officers took the last lifeboat to shore, but they returned to the steamer in the predawn hours. In *Captain Ben's Book*, Benjamin Willard, a Cape Elizabeth native and harbor pilot, described his experience upon arriving at the scene of the disaster: "When we got to the ship it was the hardest sight that I had ever looked at. We found Captain

Bolan's [*sic*] boat and crew. He seemed to be completely prostrated over the loss of his ship and the passengers."

The first passenger to arrive in Portland, J. S. Miller, passed the word of the disaster to the press. All told, forty-two people, including two crewmembers, had perished. Some men who had been attending a Washington's Birthday party at the Ocean House, a hotel in Cape Elizabeth, recovered many of the bodies. The dead were laid out under sails in the blacksmith house next to the hotel.

From all accounts, the people of Cape Elizabeth exhibited great generosity and kindness to the shipwreck victims. Many of them opened their homes and provided food and warmth for the exhausted survivors, and it was reported on the day after the wreck that local people had collected money for the aid of the passengers from the *Bohemian*. The Portland Board of Trade collected $1,500 and distributed it along with clothing to the survivors, an act that was officially recognized by the British government. Temporary living space was provided for some in Portland's new city hall.

Among the survivors was a young Irishman named John E. Fitzgerald. He was not the grandfather of President John F. Kennedy, John F. Fitzgerald, contrary to some sources; he was another man with a similar name. Fitzgerald's sister, Ellen O'Connor, described as an "active, strong young woman," was among those who died.

Another survivor, Mary Gorham, a native of Galway County, Ireland, later described being bound to a mast for hours before her rescue. She lived to the age of 101 and was the oldest resident of Lynn, Massachusetts, at the time of her death in 1895.

Just two days after the wreck, the Portland coroner conducted an inquiry, with a seven-man jury. The investigation lasted three days. When Borland's judgment was questioned, the chief saloon steward, James Hatter, testified to the captain's sobriety. Hatter said that he had brought the captain only one glass of ale that day. "He was not in the habit of drinking while at sea," said the steward.

The coroner's jury ruled that the accident was the result of an error in judgment on the part of Captain Borland, the lack of a bell on Alden's Rock, and the inattention of the pilot for not noticing the signals from the *Bohemian*. The jury also declared that, "after the vessel struck, her officers and men worked with energy and good judgment, rarely equaled and never surpassed, to avoid the loss of life."

A wrecking company was employed to salvage what it could. Some bodies were recovered, and thirty-three mailbags were saved. Only one bag of mail, intended for delivery to Philadelphia, was lost.

Despite an armed guard sent to protect the cargo, a good deal of clothing and other materials was pilfered. Eleven days after the wreck the workers had sealed the steamer and were about to pump it out. Before they could do so, an easterly gale ended the operation.

The storm broke up the remains of the *Bohemian,* strewing much debris around the vicinity. "It is hardly necessary to speak of the awful grandeur of the scene," wrote a reporter for the *Portland Advertiser.* Boxes of tea, spools of cotton, skeins of valuable silks, and other goods washed ashore along with personal items. That year, it was said, women from Cape Elizabeth to the islands of Casco Bay all had new Easter dresses.

Benjamin Willard, who worked as one of the salvagers, followed the trail of debris and managed to fill his pilot boat with recovered crates. Three more bodies also came ashore at this time: a man, a woman, and a little girl.

By late April all the bodies had been recovered. Twelve corpses that remained unclaimed were buried in a mass grave at Calvary Cemetery in South Portland. The grave remained unmarked until 1984, when two local Irish organizations, the Ancient Order of Hibernians and the Irish American Club of Portland, dedicated a large granite Celtic cross on the spot.

The Portland Board of Trade undertook a thorough examination of the area's rocks and shoals to make sure suitable buoys marked them. The wreck of the Bohemian was also a contributing factor to improvements made at Portland Head Lighthouse on Cape Elizabeth. The tower was subsequently raised twenty feet and a new, powerful second-order lens was installed.

On December 23, 1886, the three-masted Canadian schooner *Adelaide* went aground on Alden's Rock, sustaining much damage

H. M. S. BOHEMIAN
SUNK
FEB. 22. 1864

MARY McDONOUGH
PATRICK McDONOUGH
THOMAS McDONOUGH
MARY McDONOUGH
ELLEN FLAHERTY
BARBARA CANAVAN
JAMES CASIDY
ANN MULLEN
BRIDE [MARY]
THOMAS KILIAN
THOMAS CLARKE
CHILD (LITTLE GIRL)

In 1984 the Ancient Order of Hibernians and the Irish American Club of Portland dedicated a cross on the mass grave of victims from the *Bohemian* disaster. Photo by Jeremy D'Entremont.

but no casualties. Apparently, Alden's Rock still wasn't sufficiently well marked. A newspaper reporter commented, "A common can buoy is the only sign that marks the ledge. A bell or light buoy should take its place at once." The spot is marked today by a red nun buoy southwest of the rock.

The *Bohemian* tragedy is recalled in a poignant mural, *Shipwreck at Night*, painted by Alzira Peirce, on public display at the post office in South Portland.

CHAPTER SIX

The Bark *Annie C. Maguire* at Portland Head Lighthouse, 1886

WITH NO INJURIES or loss of life, the wreck of the *Annie C. Maguire* was minor as shipping disasters go. It ranks among the most famous Maine shipwrecks just the same, for one reason. It occurred right next to one of the most popular lighthouses on the East Coast, in plain sight of its keepers. Because of its proximity to the mainland lighthouse, the wreck was seen and photographed by many visitors.

Anyone who has seen the incongruous images of the once-proud tall ship stranded within a stone's throw of the iconic lighthouse is unlikely to forget it. No trace of the ship remains, but an inscription painted on the ledge informs visitors of the event: "Annie C. Maguire shipwrecked here Christmas Eve 1886."

The ship we know as the *Annie C. Maguire* led two lives. Its first incarnation was as the extreme clipper ship *Golden State,* built by the shipbuilder Jacob A. Westervelt on the East River in New York City in 1852–53. When the 188-foot clipper was launched in January 1853, it was already carrying a San Francisco–bound cargo. The *Golden State* was owned by the firm Chambers and Heiser and was a sister ship to the *Golden Gate.*

The *Golden State* was one of the fastest and most durable vessels built in the golden age of clipper ships. Narrow for their length and with a large sail area, clippers were built for speed in the days of the California Gold Rush and trade with the Far East. They were, as the maritime historian Alexander Laing wrote, "half poetry, all daring, and the most beautiful objects on the sea."

When the *Golden State* left Battery Park, Manhattan, on February 8, 1853, crowds gathered to watch the magnificent ship begin its maiden voyage to the West Coast. The clipper seemed destined to threaten the record for the shortest voyage between New York and San Francisco (set at 89 days, 8 hours, in 1853 by the *Flying Cloud*), but a windstorm tore down its three topmasts on February 18. After repairs in Rio de Janeiro, the ship sailed on to San Francisco, arriving after 133 days.

The *Golden State* had many highlights in its lifetime, including a near record-breaking eighty-nine-day voyage from Shanghai to New York in 1855. In May 1867 the ship's cargo of tea from China, which sold for $1 million, was the largest ever to arrive in New York Harbor.

The darkest days aboard the clipper occurred in 1858, when the crew mutinied over inadequate food during passage to Hong Kong. The mutineers attacked the officers, and the first mate died of his wounds. The perpetrators escaped temporarily but were later captured.

During one of the *Golden State*'s last voyages under that name, in December 1881, Captain Rowland T. Delano was credited with the rescue of nine shipwrecked Chinese sailors. The Chinese men spent a month aboard the clipper before being turned over to Chinese authorities at Kobe, Japan.

In early 1883, after an unusually long thirty-year career in the China trade, the *Golden State* was converted to bark rigging. After leaving New York in January of that year, the ship ran into a storm in the Atlantic and had to put into Rio for repairs. It was subsequently sold to the firm of D&J Maguire of Quebec, Canada.

Renamed the *Annie C. Maguire,* the vessel sailed under the British flag in North and South America during the 1883–86 period. A brief item in the *New York Times* of June 5, 1885, informs us that the bark, carrying a cargo of sugar and molasses, set a new speed record by completing a voyage from Barbados to Quebec in seventeen days.

The *Maguire* was headed home to Quebec in December 1886, after leaving Buenos Aires. On board with Captain Daniel O'Niel were his wife and twelve-year-old son, two mates, and thirteen crewmen. The *Maguire* entered Casco Bay at about eleven o'clock on Christmas Eve, with the intention of riding out some bad weather in Portland Harbor.

A heavy sea was visible outside Portland Harbor that day, as a winter storm was raging offshore. At Portland Head Lighthouse on Cape Elizabeth, a few miles from the harbor's entrance, Keeper Joshua Freeman Strout was asked by a sheriff's officer to keep an eye out for the ship, in case the captain decided to duck into Portland Harbor to take shelter from the storm.

Joshua Strout was a former sea captain who had become a lighthouse keeper at Portland Head in 1869, after a fall from a masthead forced him to give up life at sea. Joshua and his wife, Mary (Berry), raised eleven children at the station. They were no strangers to maritime tragedy; three of their sons were lost at sea during the family's years at Portland Head.

Mary Strout served as an assistant keeper until 1877, when her son Joseph Woodbury Strout was named assistant. Joseph Strout went on to succeed his father as principal keeper in 1904, and he retired in 1928 after living for fifty-nine years at Portland Head.

Joseph Strout was described as a "bronzed, hardy little man, comfortably inclined to corpulence" in a 1927 article, in which he recalled the night the *Annie C. Maguire* was wrecked. Some accounts of the event claim the weather was clear, but Joseph Strout firmly stated otherwise: "The wind was howling a gale," he said. "It was Christmas Eve, you know, and I guess even Santa Claus was afraid to be out."

Strangely, in an interview in 1929, Joseph Strout said it was snowing so hard "you couldn't see a hand in front of you," but that the night was calm and there was no wind. He said his father was on watch in the lighthouse and the "world [was] as silent as death." Windy or not, in both interviews Strout stressed the fact that it was snowing heavily.

In his booklet *Golden State/Annie C. Maguire,* Kenneth A. Moody

The *Annie C. Maguire* on the rocks at Portland Head Lighthouse.
Courtesy of the Museum at Portland Head Light.

informs us that Portland weather reports say it was 46 degrees with heavy rain that night. Moody believed that there was probably a snow squall at Cape Elizabeth. In one of the first photos taken after the wreck, he points out, what appears to be snow can be seen on the rocks.

It's generally believed that Captain O'Niel and his crew probably couldn't see the lighthouse in the squall, or they thought it was farther away than it was. It has been reported, however, that members of the crew later said they "plainly saw the light" before the disaster. A clear picture can't be drawn at this late date.

At about eleven-thirty that night, as Joshua Strout kept watch in the lighthouse tower, Joseph was preparing for bed. Suddenly, Joshua burst through the door of the keeper's house and exclaimed, "All hands turn out! There's a ship ashore in the dooryard!" Joseph fumbled as he put his socks and shoes back on and then bolted down the stairs a half dozen at a time.

When he emerged from the house, Joseph Strout was amazed to see the ship on the ledges no more than a hundred feet from the lighthouse tower, listing to one side. As soon as it had run onto the ledge, the captain had had the crew take down the sails and lower the anchors.

According to some accounts, Mary Strout shed light on the scene by burning blankets that had been cut into strips and soaked in kerosene. There are varying versions of how the Strouts rescued the people from the ship. In 1927 Joseph Strout said that the water was calm enough to permit the men "to jump ashore, almost without help, so hard on the ledge was the vessel."

According to Joseph's grandson, John Strout, in an article in *Lighthouse Digest,* Joshua and Joseph rigged a line to the *Maguire,* and they rescued everyone with a breeches buoy (a device that is explained in detail in chapter 9). Other sources claim the Strouts put a ladder across the rocks to the ship, and all aboard made it safely across the ladder to solid ground.

Kenneth A. Moody believes a ladder was the likely means of rescue. It was too short a distance to warrant a line from the shore to the ship, and there would have been a rush to get everyone off as quickly as possible in case the *Maguire* broke apart. Captain O'Niel, according to John Strout, was the last to leave the ship. Just before he came off, his sea chest was passed ashore.

Mary Strout soon had hot coffee and food ready for the shipwreck victims in an engine room. They were ravenous after their long voyage, having had little more to eat than salt beef and macaroni. Joseph Strout said in 1929:

> The day before we had killed eight chickens so that we could have a big feed on Christmas. Ma made all eight into the best pie you ever tasted. But it didn't make no impression on that crew of three-quarter starved blotters though. I only got one plateful.
>
> But we should worry. A feller doesn't get wrecked often, and when it happens where he can eat after starving for weeks, you can't blame him for passing his plate until it's all gone.
>
> Once they got that chicken pie into them, the whole gang wanted to stay. They loafed around three days and ate most of

the food we had while Dad did his best to convince them that we were a lighthouse and not a life saving station.

On Christmas morning, a deputy sheriff made his way to the lighthouse to present papers of attachment to Captain O'Niel. The attachment was on behalf of a Boston bank, Kidder, Peabody and Company, a creditor of D&J Maguire, owners of the *Annie C. Maguire.* The company had failed, one of many during an economic downturn at the time.

According to Bill Caldwell's *Islands of Maine,* the authorities searched a sea chest from the *Maguire* for the ship's papers. When the captain realized that a satchel containing the papers along with his and the ship's money was missing, he frantically informed his wife. She told her husband to keep quiet and pretend the satchel had been lost in the wreck. In fact, she had taken all the cash and papers, and they were well hidden in her hatbox.

Some sources have suggested that the ship was heavily insured, and that Captain O'Niel might have wrecked it on purpose to collect insurance money. This seems unlikely. The *Maguire* was only

Joshua Freeman Strout was the principal keeper at Portland Head Light 1869–1904. Courtesy of the Museum at Portland Head Light.

The *Annie C. Maguire* inscription is still repainted on the rocks from time to time. Photo by Jeremy D'Entremont.

partially insured, and it's doubtful that O'Niel would have risked the lives of his wife and son—along with his own—for insurance money.

Joshua Strout was put in charge of the ship by the deputy sheriff, and the wreck was soon surveyed. The *New York Times* reported on December 27 that the *Maguire*'s bottom was "badly stove." It was thought that the ship would probably break apart in the next storm, so Joshua Strout ordered that everything removable be brought ashore as quickly as possible.

Among the items salvaged were two cases of Scotch whiskey. According to Joseph Strout, the crewmen drank themselves senseless and proceeded to beat up the ship's cook as punishment for the subpar rations he had served on their voyage.

The *Maguire* broke apart in a storm about a week after the wreck. Joseph Strout kept a souvenir from the ship for himself, and he was always happy to explain it to visitors. It was a boarding pike, described as looking like a Roman spear, and "used probably to bust some poor native's head when he tried to the board the ship," according to Strout. "The natives used to bother the old vessels some."

Less than a year after the *Maguire* wreck, on November 30, 1887, the schooner *D. W. Hammond* was driven ashore at Portland Head in a severe northeaster. Joseph Strout and his brother Gilman braved the storm to pull the captain and two crewmen to safety.

Another wreck, that of the schooner *Lochinvar*, took place in fog on October 4, 1932, only about a hundred feet from the spot where the *Maguire* struck. The cargo of 40,000 pounds of fish was lost, but the captain and crew escaped.

Joseph Strout's son, John A. Strout (father of the author of the *Lighthouse Digest* article), was born at the lighthouse in 1891. He followed the family tradition by becoming an assistant keeper under his father, on his twenty-first birthday. On the same day John A. Strout painted an inscription on the ledge where the *Maguire* was wrecked. He first had to chip much of the huge rock to make a flat surface on which to paint, and the lettering was applied with a mixture of paint, mortar, and sand.

The exact wording and spelling of the inscription have varied over the years, and a wooden cross that once topped the rock is gone, but the tradition of repainting it continues as a reminder of the night a once-proud ship almost hit the lighthouse.

CHAPTER SEVEN

The Strange Loss of the *Don*, 1941

IT WAS A SUNNY early morning on Sunday, June 29, 1941, as Paul Johnson of East Harpswell prepared his boat, the cabin cruiser *Don,* for a pleasure trip to Monhegan Island for a lobster bake. The *Don,* with thirty-four people aboard, would never reach Monhegan. The mysterious loss ranks as one of Maine's greatest maritime tragedies of the twentieth century.

Stacy L. Welner, a writer based in Harpswell, became fascinated by the *Don* mystery, and she published her extensively researched book *Tragedy in Casco Bay* in 2006. Many of the facts cited in this chapter are from Welner's book. "We'll probably never know what really happened," Welner told the *Portland Press Herald.* "I think it's important to tell this story. The people who were on that boat need not be forgotten."

The forty-four-foot *Don* was freshly painted, and Johnson, with the help of his friend Joseph Bernier, had checked the condition of all the life jackets. Some had been borrowed from Bernier's boat, for a total of forty on board. The battery had been charged a week earlier and repairs had been completed to the gasoline tank. It would be the first excursion of the year for the *Don.*

Johnson, a forty-five-year-old veteran fisherman and lobsterman, had plied the waters of Casco Bay from boyhood and was regarded by most as a fine skipper, but locals thought the *Don*— bought by Johnson in 1940—was a "patch job." The boat, built in the "Nova Scotian" style around 1900, had undergone many modifications and had been used as a rumrunner in the days of Prohibition.

State Fisheries Warden John Stevens said later that the *Don* was considered top-heavy; it had sunk on two or three previous occasions with no passengers on board. Stevens had been on the boat not long before the fateful voyage, and the smell of gasoline was so strong that he quickly tossed his lit cigar into the ocean. It was also reported that the *Don* had been carelessly left out in the ice all the preceding winter.

The passengers out for a day of fun came from the towns of Rumford and Mexico, neighboring Maine communities on the Androscoggin River, about sixty miles north of Portland. Some were employees of the Oxford Paper Mill in Rumford. Many in the group had enjoyed a cruise with Johnson the previous year, and they were looking forward to doing it again. Johnson was also happily anticipating the trip; he had told his housekeeper that the group was his favorite.

Albert Melanson, a clerk at the Rumford Falls Trust Company, organized the Monhegan trip. In a letter to Johnson a few days earlier, Melanson had written, "One of the mermaids has made a bet with me that we wouldn't reach Monhegan. Hope I don't lose out." There were several family groups on the cruise; Melanson brought his two teenage sons with him, as well as his brother, Alban.

Along for the trip was a deckhand, Norman Foster, who was filling in for his younger brother, Robert. Robert Foster decided to go herring fishing instead of boarding the *Don* that morning. Norman Foster's fiancée, Ramola Brundage of California, also went on the cruise.

The eager excursionists gathered at Dyers Cove, an indentation of the craggy peninsula that constitutes East Harpswell, intending to get started at eight o'clock that morning. Dr. Oscar Miller and his wife, residents of Livermore Falls, got on board, but Miller's visiting brother and sister-in-law changed their minds at the last minute and stayed onshore.

As Joseph Bernier helped Johnson with the preparations, he saw one of the arriving passengers, a young woman, throw a beach ball on board the *Don*. The trip got started somewhere between eight-thirty and nine-thirty.

The *Don*, in a view from the Record of Investigation of the Bureau of Marine Inspection and Navigation. Courtesy of Stacy L. Welner.

Johnson navigated the *Don* out of the cove. Witnesses later said they saw the boat passing near Great Island, a short distance from the cove, at about nine-thirty. It was reported that many of the passengers were riding on top of the cabin, causing the prow to dip low in the water.

After traveling about six miles, the party landed briefly at West Point, near Cape Small in Phippsburg. Some of the passengers visited Reed's General Store. Johnson bought some onions and potatoes at the store for the chowder he intended to make. According to *Time* magazine, he also bought lobsters in the store. It was slightly after ten o'clock, and Johnson told the storekeeper he expected to arrive at Monhegan, more than thirty miles from East Harpswell, at one o'clock.

At the store, a few passengers mailed postcards to family and friends. Beatrice Roach, twenty years old, sent a card to her mother that read, "Feeling fine, not seasick. But there is still 30 more miles to go, Bea." Leila Sanders wrote to a friend, "No casualties yet!"

The *Don* passed a workboat, the *Manela*, at ten-fifty. The boat's owner, Alvin Brewer, said later that ten or fifteen women were riding on top of the cabin. Brewer and Johnson shouted to each other to make sure both understood which way they would pass.

At about eleven-forty Maxwell DeShon, second assistant keeper at the Seguin Island Light Station, off the mouth of the Kennebec River, watched the *Don* pass south of the island, some of its passengers still riding on top of the cabin. The weather was increasingly hazy as DeShon observed the boat heading in the direction of the rocks known as the Cuckolds, toward Boothbay Harbor, not Monhegan. That was the last time anyone would see the *Don* afloat, or any of its passengers alive. F. E. Singer, keeper at the Cuckolds Lighthouse, later said that he never saw the vessel near his station.

Joseph Bernier noticed a beach ball floating near Flat Ledge around two or two-thirty. He recognized it as the same ball he had seen a passenger throw on board the *Don* that morning.

By that night relatives and friends grew worried when there was no sign of the *Don*. The Damariscove Island Coast Guard Station was alerted in the predawn hours of Monday morning. Captain Milton H. Seavy made inquiries of other stations and local harbors, but no one had seen the missing boat. Seavy set out in a utility boat with two other Coast Guardsmen, but dense fog rendered their efforts futile.

Seavy followed what he believed would have been Paul Johnson's route. He spoke with lighthouse keepers and fishermen at Monhegan, who said the *Don* had never arrived there. Seavy took the search to Pemaquid Point and Boothbay Harbor, up the Sheepscot River to Five Islands, then to Bath and Seguin Island. He returned to Damariscove Island after ten hours of fruitless searching, as darkness fell and the fog hung thick.

The passengers' loved ones congregated near the eleven empty cars left by the missing at Dyer's Cove, and a woman's home nearby became a makeshift headquarters. *Time* magazine described a "throng of weeping kinfolk" gathered at the cove. The fog lifted slightly by Tuesday morning, and the search resumed.

A short time later hopes were crushed when the bodies of two female passengers, Dorcas Kersey and Bessie Strople, were discovered floating off Bailey Island. Claude Johnson, a Bailey Island fisherman, found the first body. The body of Elizabeth Howard was soon found in the same area.

Twenty-year-old Beatrice E. Roach, left, of Rumford, was engaged to Harry C. Hutchins, right. Both of them died aboard the *Don*. Courtesy of Stacy L. Welner.

By late Wednesday it had become apparent that no one had survived, and the search was called off. Flags at the town halls in Rumford and Mexico were lowered to half-mast. In addition to the Coast Guard, state police, and fisheries personnel, more than one hundred private boats had taken part in the search. The loss of thirty-four lives made this the worst maritime tragedy New England had experienced in sixteen years.

On July 1 the *Portsmouth Herald* reported, "Recovery of five women's bodies, one of them burned, gave mute evidence today the cabin cruiser *Don* had gone down in lower Casco Bay after an explosion." Fourteen bodies were eventually recovered by mid-July, scattered to the south all the way to Biddeford Pool, more than twenty miles south of Harpswell. None of them was wearing life jackets, which indicated that they were the victims of a sudden calamity.

Watches were found on several of the victims, stopped between 11:35 and 11:43. This would seem to indicate that the disaster occurred in the late morning, shortly after the *Don* was sighted from Seguin Island. There were sketchy reports, however, that the vessel actually arrived at Monhegan and was seen returning late in the afternoon. A keeper at Seguin Island thought he'd seen the *Don* pass about seven o'clock on Sunday evening, heading toward Damariscove Island.

The body of Paul Johnson was discovered with a rope securely around his waist and a keg (used as a fishing buoy) at the other end; he had apparently tried to save himself by this measure. Most of the *Don* itself was missing, but some wreckage was recovered. Much of the wheelhouse floated ashore.

Newspaper reports mentioned charred spots on the wreckage, which might have indicated a fire or explosion. The *New York Times* reported that Coast Guard Lieutenant Thomas Sampson was convinced that the *Don* had "undoubtedly" exploded, the reason being the discovery of burns on the victims and the "charred marks" on the vessel's wheelhouse.

Dr. Earle Richardson, the medical examiner for Cumberland County, believed that what were at first thought to be burns on the victims were actually the result of "skin crawling," or water burns, which typically occurs if a body is in the water for more than twenty-four hours. Some of the bodies exhibited bruises, apparently sustained when they struck rocks or the shore. No autopsies were performed because none of the families consented.

On July 6, a week after the disaster, hundreds of mourners gathered at Chisholm Park in Rumford for a memorial service. Among the speakers at the gathering was Maine's Governor Sumner Sewall.

At the same time, services were held for a large crowd on a wharf at Bailey Island, part of the town of Harpswell. The crew of the Sea and Shore Fisheries boat *Maine* dropped flowers into the sea nearby as a flag onshore was lowered to half-mast. After the playing of taps, mourners tossed wreaths and flowers into the water. Only a fraction of the attendees were able to crowd inside the small Bailey Island chapel for the service that followed.

Two weeks after the disaster, Governor Sewall appointed a Maine board of inquiry made up of local officials. A second investigation was conducted in late July by a federal board that included Coast Guard officials. The official ruling was that all died by accidental drowning after the *Don* capsized in a groundswell because of its inherent instability and the weight of the passengers.

Some of the bodies were found near Little Mark Island, about two miles southwest of Bailey Island. The island is home to a navigational marker built in 1827. Photo by Jeremy D'Entremont.

Not everyone agreed. Paul C. Thurston, president of the Rumford Falls Trust Company, where some of the victims had worked, believed there had been an explosion caused by problems with the gas tank. It was a known fact that the tank had undergone recent repairs. Thurston believed that a gas leak produced gasoline in the bilge and fumes in the cabin, and that an explosion had immediately resulted when Johnson lit a fire to cook his chowder.

The popular New England historian Edward Rowe Snow wrote about the *Don* in his books *New England Sea Tragedies* (1960) and *The Romance of Casco Bay* (1975). As he often did in his colorful career, Snow took a personal interest in the story. After reports that wreckage from the *Don* may have been found in 1958, Snow organized diving expeditions in 1959 and 1960. Nothing more was found.

Snow received many letters concerning the *Don* over the years, and some of them claimed special knowledge of what really happened to the *Don*. One writer claimed that unidentified persons had the *Don* sunk deliberately as part of some kind of obscure plot.

Another letter writer insisted that a German U-boat, which had been hiding in Casco Bay waiting to attack the next vessel that came along, sank the cabin cruiser. This seems unlikely, as German submarines weren't commonly seen in the waters of New England until after the United States entered World War II at the end of 1941. Another person wrote to Snow that the *Don* had been sunk by a wayward underwater mine that had drifted from its moorings near Halifax, Nova Scotia.

In *New England Sea Tragedies,* Snow wrote, "I have heard so many rumors from so many sources, that I now believe that the entire affair, horrible as it is to say so, was planned from beginning to end. There are greater forces than we can understand at the back of the disaster, and the average person will never know the truth which has been known for some time by certain residents of Casco Bay."

A June 1997 article in *Down East* magazine revealed the identity of the writer of a "conspiracy theory" letter mailed to Snow. It was the wife of Paul Johnson's friend Joseph Bernier. She claimed that her husband had twice previously burned boats to collect the insurance, and she suspected his involvement in the *Don* disaster.

In early August 1963 what may have been the bow of the *Don* was found and recovered by two dragger fishermen near Round Rock in Casco Bay. Items including footwear were still intact inside the bow. A pair of opera glasses that bore the initials "L.S." was believed to have belonged to Leila Sanders.

The material was never proven to be from the *Don* and it was thrown back, but the find lent credence to the theory that the *Don* went down at about eleven-forty on June 29, about an hour after it left West Point. The boat's average speed would have put it near Round Rock at around eleven-thirty.

Another local fisherman had heard, around the time of the *Don*'s disappearance, the racing of the boat's engine at Round Rock Ledge, where he believed it had run aground. The witness said that the motor raced violently, as if Johnson was desperately trying to get the *Don* off the ledge. There were also reports of copper paint found on the ropes of another fisherman when he fished near Round Rock.

Stacy Welner, the author of *Tragedy in Casco Bay,* believes that the *Don* capsized. Someone in the area, she theorizes, would have heard an explosion if one had taken place.

The tragedy and mystery surrounding the disappearance of the *Don* continue to intrigue and inspire. A novel by Peter Landesman, *The Raven,* published in 1997, is loosely based on the story of the *Don.* In 2008 the Maine composers Peter J. McLaughlin and Akiva G. Zamcheck memorialized the tragedy in a work for guitar and percussion called *Shipwreck off Casco Bay.* A one-hour documentary film, *Gone: The Mystery of the Don Disaster,* directed by Dave Wilkinson and produced by Marilyn Taylor, was completed in 2009.

Precisely what happened in the final moments of the *Don* will never be known. If foul play was involved and any living persons know the true facts, they aren't talking.

CHAPTER EIGHT

The Sinking of
the USS *Eagle 56*, 1945

IT MAY SURPRISE many Americans to learn that German U-boats sank more than six hundred American military and merchant vessels in the Atlantic between January and August 1942, with little fear of reprisal. For the U-boat commanders it was the "Second Happy Time" or the "Great American Turkey Shoot." Winston Churchill later wrote, "The only thing that ever really frightened me during the war was the U-boat peril."

The American military response was slow, and the public was shielded by wartime censorship from the gravity of the situation. Witnesses to sinkings were asked to remain silent as part of the effort to keep civilian morale at a high level.

The use of convoys across the Atlantic, coastal blackouts, the breaking of the German code, and stepped-up military production all led to the containment of the U-boat threat. By 1943 American air and sea power had grown to the point that a successful offensive was launched against the U-boats. This turning of the tide eventually gave the Allied nations control of the shipping lanes and allowed the invasion of occupied Europe. Still, the threat of attack by German submarines remained very real until the end of the war.

When the USS *Eagle 56* was destroyed by a torpedo fired by the German submarine *U-583* on April 23, 1945, taking with it the lives of forty-nine men, it was the greatest loss of life in any incident in New England waters during World War II. Coming just two weeks before Germany surrendered and occurring relatively close to shore, the sinking was an embarrassment to the U.S. Navy—so much so that it took more than a half century for the truth to be told. Stephen Puleo has chronicled the entire tale in engrossing detail in his book *Due to Enemy Action.*

The Eagle class of U.S. Navy boats was developed during World War I, when a need was recognized for vessels that would be smaller and more maneuverable than destroyers, but faster and more fuel-efficient than the 110-foot wooden-hulled submarine chasers then in use. The name "Eagle boat" was adopted after an editorial in the *Washington Post* called for "an eagle to scour the seas and pounce upon and destroy every German submarine." Their official name was "PE boats," for patrol escort.

President Woodrow Wilson brought in Henry Ford as a consultant, and the Ford Motor Company established a factory to produce Eagle boats in Detroit. Modern mass-production techniques were utilized; the three assembly lines were each a third of a mile long. The large workforce peaked at eight thousand. The first of the two-hundred-foot steel-hulled ships was launched in July 1918. In all, sixty Eagle boats were launched in 1918–19. The original contract had called for one hundred, but Ford learned that shipbuilding was more difficult than he had imagined.

The Eagle boats failed miserably as sub chasers. The maritime historian Samuel Eliot Morison wrote that they were "square-built, slow, weak," and "almost completely useless." They never saw duty in World War I. Some were transferred to the Coast Guard, and some were used as aircraft tenders in the 1920s. Only eight were still in service by the dawn of World War II.

Among the last to be completed was the *Eagle 56,* launched on the Detroit River on August 15, 1919. The *Eagle 56* became part of the Naval Reserve force in Washington, D.C., between 1921 and 1926, and it was then used as a Naval Reserve training ship in Baltimore.

On February 28, 1942, German torpedoes sunk the destroyer USS *Jacob Jones II* off the coast of Delaware. The vigilant crew of the *Eagle 56,* which was based at Cape May, New Jersey, at the time, plucked a dozen survivors from life rafts. A short time later, the *Eagle 56* sustained damage in a collision with the submerged British

The USS *Eagle 2* (PE-2), seen here during a trial run in 1918, was an identical sister ship to the USS *Eagle 56* (PE-56). U.S. Navy photo.

ship *Gypsum Prince* while rescuing survivors after the freighter had been torpedoed.

After repairs, the *Eagle 56* became a training ship at a sonar school in Key West in May 1942. During the following year the vessel was involved in the development of antisubmarine torpedoes.

The *Eagle 56* arrived at its final port at Portland, Maine, in the summer of 1944. Portland, with a strong U.S. Navy presence, was a busy place during the war. Just across the harbor, in South Portland, nearly thirty thousand people worked at shipyards that produced more than two hundred of the cargo-carrying Liberty ships that were so vital to the war effort.

At Portland the primary job of the crew of the *Eagle 56* was to tow a target float off Cape Elizabeth, so that navy and marine bomber pilots could practice their aim before leaving for the Pacific. Many of the crewmen had seen action in the Pacific and North Africa, and serving on a target ship was considered an easy way to finish the war. The *Eagle 56*'s captain was Lieutenant Commander James G. Early.

Some of the crew of the USS *Eagle 56* are seen here at Key West, Florida, before they left for Portland, Maine. Standing at the far left is John Scagnelli. Second from left in the front row is Harold Petersen. John Breeze is the second from left in the second row. Joseph Priestas, the fourth survivor of the 1945 sinking, is the third from the left in the second row. From the book *Due to Enemy Action*, courtesy of Stephen Puleo.

A few German subs still lingered close to the U.S. coastline during the war's final weeks. On April 11, 1945, the day before President Franklin D. Roosevelt died and less than a month before German forces surrendered, Admiral Karl Dönitz, commander of the German naval forces, sent a message to his U-boat commanders. "No one thinks of giving up his ship," he told them. "Rather, go down in honor." The order was to "fight to the end."

During most of April 1945 a German U-boat in the Gulf of Maine was tracked at the "Secret Room" in Washington, D.C., where all U-boat positions were plotted. The tracking grew difficult, as the U-boat sent and received few communications.

The submarine they were watching was the *U-853*, with fifty-five men aboard. The commander was Helmut Frömsdorf, twenty-four years old and ambitious. In his final letter to his parents, Frömsdorf wrote, "I am lucky in these difficult days of my fatherland to have the honor of commanding this submarine. . . . I'm not very good at last words."

April 23 began as a routine day for the crewmen of the *Eagle 56*. Machinist's Mate First Class Harold Glenn hurried to catch the bus from his home to the Portland waterfront. As Puleo's book poignantly describes, Glenn asked the driver to wait. He ran back up the stairs to his apartment. When his wife asked what was wrong, Glenn said he had forgotten to kiss her good-bye. Esta Glenn would never see her husband after their quick kiss that morning.

A little past noon that day the *U-853* drew within six hundred yards of the *Eagle 56* as it sat at a dead stop about three miles offshore. It was an easy mark for the U-boat. A torpedo fired by the *U-853* ran swiftly into the *Eagle 56* on the starboard side. The boat was ripped in half, and the resulting geyser of water was reported to be at least two hundred feet high. The explosion was seen as far away as Fort Williams and Portland Head Lighthouse on Cape Elizabeth, nine miles distant, and was heard by residents of Portland.

All the men on the bridge and almost all the men below deck in the bow section were killed. Survivors leaped into the water to escape the sinking wreckage. Some of the men later said that they saw the dark shape of a submarine conning tower rise out of the sea, bearing the distinctive insignia of a red horse on a yellow shield.

The engineering officer, Lieutenant John Scagnelli, was the only man who escaped the bow section alive. Scagnelli was knocked from the bunk in his cabin and suffered a deep scalp wound. "I was thrown just as if someone had picked me up and tossed me," he said later.

Scagnelli reached the deck just in time to see the bow, where he had been resting peacefully moments earlier, sink beneath the surface with many of his fellow crewmen still inside. Cletus Frane was being pulled down by the suction of the sinking vessel when a wooden Coke case bumped into him; it served as a life preserver. Daniel Jaronik held tightly to part of the target buoy the men had deployed before the explosion.

Minutes before the attack, Harold Petersen had been relieved of his engine room watch by Fred Michelsen. Michelsen died instantly, but Petersen, who had gone to the aft section, escaped with his life as he dove into the cold sea.

Petersen, Scagnelli, and the other survivors treaded water as they waited for rescue ships to arrive. Scagnelli and two other men, Johnny Breeze and John Luttrell, clung desperately to a floating oil tank, which soon sank. Petersen found a floating piece of wood and maneuvered it close enough so that Scagnelli, Breeze, and Luttrell were able to grab on to it. Some of the survivors later praised Petersen and Scagnelli for their heroic conduct in the crisis.

Most of the survivors were suffering from hypothermia by the time they were pulled from the ocean into a whaleboat by the crew of the destroyer USS *Selfridge,* almost twenty minutes after the explosion.

Some of the other men who escaped the *Eagle 56* couldn't hold on long enough. As the first group of survivors was transferred from the whaleboat to the *Selfridge,* sharp sonar echoes indicated that a U-boat was lurking close by. The captain gave orders to start the engines. As the ship's screws began to turn, some of the men still in the water were sucked to their deaths. "The captain had no choice," said one of the *Selfridge* crewmen later. Several depth charges were dropped, but there was no hit.

The crew of the Nantucket Lightship (LV-112), which was used as an examination vessel at Portland during the war, arrived on the scene just after the *Selfridge* and plucked Harold Petersen from the waves. Only thirteen men aboard the *Eagle 56* escaped with their lives, and forty-nine men died—five officers and forty-four enlisted men.

At the Navy's Secret Room, Commander Kenneth Knowles received the message: "Eagle 56 exploded and sunk from unknown cause. Possibly by U-boat." Because of the wartime censorship that was then in effect, nothing about the explosion appeared in newspapers until May 9. The *Portland Press Herald* called it a "mysterious boat blast." The *New York Times* of May 9 noted that some of the survivors believed they had seen a submarine, but it added that

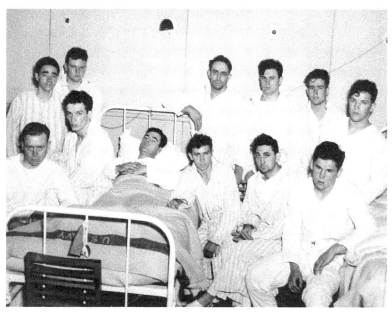

Twelve of the "lucky thirteen" survivors of the sinking of the USS *Eagle 56* shortly after their rescue. From the book *Due to Enemy Action*, courtesy of Stephen Puleo.

rescuers might have mistaken a part of the *Eagle 56*'s hull for a submarine in the minutes after the explosion.

A number of ships patrolled the Maine coast in search of U-boats in the days after the attack on the *Eagle 56*. The USS *Muskegon* dropped depth charges, which had no positive results, after detecting a probable submarine on the bottom on April 25. The following day an air squadron from the Quonset Naval Air Station in Rhode Island dropped two five-hundred-pound depth charges at an enemy submarine that had been spotted on the surface. The ocean was filled with oil and debris, which led the pilots to believe they had hit their target. If it was indeed the *U-853*, they had missed and the debris was a decoy.

Adolph Hitler committed suicide on April 30, 1945, and Admiral Dönitz was named his successor as president of Nazi Germany. All German forces were ordered to surrender on May 4, and an order went out to all U-boat commanders: "Cease fire at once. Stop all hostile action against Allied shipping. Dönitz." The order went into effect at eight o'clock the following morning. It isn't known if Helmut Frömsdorf, commander of the *U-853*, ever received the message.

A collier, the SS *Black Point,* was cruising along the Rhode Island coast on its way to Boston on May 5, carrying a cargo of eight thousand tons of coal and a crew of forty-one merchant seamen and five armed guards. At five-forty in the afternoon, as the collier was passing within three miles of the Point Judith Lighthouse, it was struck in the stern by a torpedo fired by the *U-853*.

The collier's captain, Charles Prior, a native of South Portland, was about to light a cigarette when the torpedo struck. He later said, "I can't remember whether I lit that cigarette, or swallowed it." The *Black Point* sank in fifteen minutes, taking with it the lives of twelve men.

Ten American ships soon arrived to surround the submarine. Near midnight that night, U.S. Navy and Coast Guard vessels located the *U-853* using sonar. Depth charges were dropped and debris was sighted, but the U-boat continued moving. The bombardment continued through the night, and two navy blimps deployed rocket bombs that broke the submarine's hull.

"There was no doubt that by this time we knew we had it," said a navy commander, "but it seemed everyone wanted to get into the act. I don't think there is a hull that took a bigger beating during the war." The next morning a diver confirmed that the U-boat had been sunk. Bodies were seen inside the badly damaged hull.

Six hours after the sinking of the *U-853* was confirmed, German forces surrendered. Frömsdorf and his crew, who may or may not have received the recent order to cease fighting, had taken to heart the earlier command to fight to the end. The crews of many other U-boats gave themselves up to the Allies following Germany's surrender.

In the days after the *Eagle 56* explosion, the families of the victims were told simply that the men had been lost at sea. A U.S. Navy court of inquiry convened on April 26, three days after the disaster. In charge of the proceedings was Commander Ernest J. Freeman, the officer in charge of the navy's operations in Portland.

The ultimate verdict, that a boiler explosion sank the *Eagle 56*, seems to have been decided before the inquiry began. There was no evidence of boiler problems; the engines had just been overhauled and the crew had tested the boiler. Lieutenant Guy V. Emro of the Coast Guard, the commander of the Nantucket Lightship, testified that he had witnessed a geyser that reached 250 or 300 feet immediately after the explosion. He believed that the blast could have been caused only by something outside the ship, not by a boiler malfunction.

The testimony of Daniel Jaronik should have proved beyond any doubt the presence of the *U-853*. He described the red and yellow insignia on the conning tower, something no American could have known about unless he had seen the submarine. The officers and sonar operators of the *Selfridge* were not invited to present their important testimony, and the court of inquiry knew nothing of the tracking of a German U-boat in the Secret Room in the days before the attack.

The official pronouncement on the *Eagle 56* disaster was released on May 2, 1945. "The only plausible conclusion that this court can logically reach is that the explosion in this case was in the boiler," wrote Judge Advocate Norman Kaufmann. "There was no fire, smoke, flame, or flying debris such as would have been present had the ship been torpedoed."

Many years later, Harold Petersen spoke of carrying a great burden for decades: "Did I do something?" he wondered. "Were we negligent? Did we kill all those men?"

John Scagnelli later expressed his opinion that the local navy officials were embarrassed that an enemy warship had penetrated so close to Portland's harbor, and they didn't want the public to know that German U-boats were still operating near the New England shore. In his book Stephen Puleo speculated that Commander Freeman might have feared a court-martial for losing a ship so close to shore when Germany was on the verge of surrender.

Fifty-three years after the sinking, in March 1998, a thirty-eight-year-old lawyer named Paul Lawton sat in Doyle's Pub and Grill in Brockton, Massachusetts, with his friends the Westerlund brothers,

Paul and Bob. Lawton's hobby was the study of German U-boats, and his articles on the subject were published widely. He didn't know that the Westerlund brothers' father, Ivar Westerlund, was among the men who died on the *Eagle 56* more than a half century earlier. The brothers had been raised by their stepfather, and Lawton knew nothing of their biological father.

The Westerlunds and Lawton were scuba divers, and Bob Westerlund suggested diving on the *U-853* in Rhode Island. It was, after all, he pointed out, the submarine that had sunk his father's ship. This was of great interest to Lawton, who knew that according to U.S. Navy records, not a single military vessel was sunk by German U-boats in New England waters.

Lawton launched a quest that didn't end until its positive conclusion in 2002. There was a setback when Lawton requested the records of the court of inquiry, and he was informed that the records were "presumed lost." In 1999, with the help of a retired navy captain, Edward J. Melanson, the "lost" records were obtained.

After he interviewed some of the living survivors, Lawton was more convinced than ever that the *Eagle 56* was almost certainly torpedoed by the *U-853*. In the summer of 2000 Lawton led an expedition to locate the remains of the *Eagle 56*. The search was fruitless, but the effort soon gained steam with the help of Representative Joseph Moakley of Massachusetts.

In the fall of 2000 the Naval Historical Center agreed to reexamine the case. After a few months the center's senior archivist, Bernard Cavalcante, determined that the *Eagle 56* had been sunk "by enemy action," and he recommended that the survivors be awarded the Purple Heart Medal. In late 2001 the secretary of the navy concurred. It was a victory for the truth, Lawton declared.

On June 8, 2002, at ten o'clock in the morning, a ceremony was held aboard the USS *Salem* in Quincy, Massachusetts. Relatives of the *Eagle 56* crew from around the country attended, along with Paul Lawton and the three remaining survivors: Harold Petersen, Johnny Breeze, and John Scagnelli. Lawton read the names of the Purple Heart recipients as each was awarded, most of them posthumously presented to relatives.

As the only surviving officer, Scagnelli had the emotional duty of reading the names of those who died. Not surprisingly, he was unable to complete the list, as memories of his shipmates flooded into his mind. Petersen and Breeze tolled the *Salem*'s bell for each of the victims. Taps was played and a wreath was laid, and the survivors presented Lawton with a handsome plaque in gratitude for his dedication. "We thank you from the bottom of our hearts," it said.

A fourth living survivor, Joseph Priestas, came forward later. In 2005 a plaque memorializing the *Eagle 56* disaster was installed near Portland Head Lighthouse in Cape Elizabeth.

Further efforts to find the remains of the *Eagle 56* on the bottom of Casco Bay have proven fruitless. The remains of the *U-853*, seven nautical miles off the northern end of Block Island in water more than one hundred feet deep, have provided an interesting but dangerous dive site for recreational divers. The spot is marked on navigation charts, "DANGER—Unexploded depth charge May 1945."

When he was notified of the reversal of the navy's official stance on the sinking of the *Eagle 56*, John Scagnelli, then eighty years old, put it all in perspective. "This puts an end to all the questions," he said. "In those days we didn't know if we were coming home or not. The men who didn't—they are the heroes."

CHAPTER NINE

The *Oakey L. Alexander*
Rescue, 1947

THE FEROCIOUS northeast storm of March 3, 1947, produced a record 4.3-foot storm surge in Portland, Maine—a foot higher than the surge experienced during Hurricane Carol, which would devastate the state in 1954. The barometer reading dipped lower than it had in the great hurricane of 1938 and the memorable Portland Gale of 1898. Many residents in the vicinity of Portland and Cape Elizabeth lost their electric power as lines went down in the strong winds, which reached eighty miles per hour.

The 1947 gale created havoc along much of the Maine coast. At Pond Island Lighthouse, off the mouth of the Kennebec River, waves broke over the roof of the residence where Keeper Napoleon B. Fickett lived, about fifty feet above the sea. At Goat Island Lighthouse off Cape Porpoise, a boardwalk, boat slip, and fence were destroyed as seas broke over the island. A fog bell tower was swept away at Saddleback Lighthouse in Penobscot Bay.

At Rockland Harbor, the ninety-five-foot dragger *Vandal* broke loose from the shipyard where it was undergoing repairs, taking forty feet of dock with it before it struck another vessel and sank. A sixty-five-foot mail boat went aground at Owls Head. Two men died when their fishing boat, the *Pemaquid 2,* was wrecked; pieces of the vessel came ashore at Old Orchard Beach. Two homes were swept out to sea at Popham Beach.

More than twenty miles off the coast, the crew of the 2,227-ton, 261-foot gypsum freighter *Novadoc* was engaged in a life-and-death struggle against the raging seas. A distress call was received from Captain A. J. Vallis of the *Novadoc* at 2:48 that morning: "NOVADOC IN TROUBLE WE ARE TWENTY TWO MILES EAST OF PORTLAND SHIPPING WATER INTO A BROKEN HATCH AND RUNNING BEFORE THE WIND."

Early in the morning Coast Guardsmen at Cape Elizabeth saw distress rockets in the distance. The Coast Guard vessel *Cowslip* was swiftly dispatched, but nothing was found. Three search planes covered 10,000 square miles of ocean to no avail. Twenty-four lives were lost, including those of two female cooks.

The *Oakey L. Alexander*, a 395-foot steamer built in 1915 at Camden, New Jersey, owned by the Pocahontas Steamship Company and named for its president, was carrying 8,200 tons of coal from Norfolk, Virginia, to Portland, with thirty-two men on board. The collier had made over eight hundred trips between the South and Portland without incident, but this was no ordinary storm.

The *Alexander* crew had been battling the storm all the way from the Cape Cod Canal. In the predawn hours of March 3, the collier was rolling in heavy seas about eight miles from Portland. The captain, fifty-three-year-old Raymond Lewis, First Mate John G. Walker, and Quartermaster Clifford Watts struggled to make out the flash of the Portland Lightship, about five miles southeast of Cape Elizabeth, through the mix of snow, rain, and sleet.

When they finally sighted the gleam in the distance, the *Alexander* crew had no way of knowing that the lightship had been dragged several miles off its station and was being battered by thirty-foot waves. Similar seas were smashing against the *Alexander*.

At about four-thirty in the morning, a particularly monstrous wave struck the collier. Only two men, Captain Lewis and a seaman, Rodney Turner, were eyewitnesses to the disastrous events that followed. Lewis later described the wave as about eighty feet high. A portion of the bow end, 135 feet long according to the captain's log entry, split from the rest of the ship.

For a few minutes, Turner said later, the bow held together and "moved up and down like it was elastic." It then broke off from the ship with a terrific noise and immediately sank beneath the waves.

Miraculously, no crewmen were in that part of the ship. One of the two lifeboats, which were hanging forty feet above the water, was also swept away, and the other lifeboat was thrown onto the deck with tremendous force.

The men's hearts stopped with the expectation that the rest of the ship would quickly follow the bow to the bottom. But it didn't sink. The *Alexander* had recently had a new bulkhead installed, just aft of the area where the bow split off. The bulkhead prevented the rest of the ship from flooding.

Realizing his good fortune, Captain Lewis ordered the crew to stand by and announced that they would steam straight for the shore of Cape Elizabeth. "I'll call you three minutes before I think she'll hit," Lewis told his crew.

The situation appeared grim. Interviewed after the storm, the boatswain, Basil Turner, said, "I wouldn't give a nickel for seeing Portland again." Manuel Pardo, the third engineer, said simply, "I thought we were goners." In spite of their fears, the men continued to do their jobs. "No one will ever have a crew as calm as mine," said Lewis. "Every man stood by his post." One of the crewmen, George S. York of Freeport, Maine, interviewed in 1997, returned the compliment. According to York, Captain Lewis's tone remained calm through the emergency.

The chief engineer, Winfield S. Brower, was a fifty-year-old native of Portland and a twenty-year employee of the Pocahontas Steamship Company. He and his two assistants, William Simpson and Arthur Bradley, took their posts in the engine room, knowing they would be the first to die if the ship began to sink. For more than an hour, they did all they could to keep the *Alexander* steaming ahead.

As the *Alexander* moved through the darkness toward the Cape Elizabeth shore, the officers took turns sounding five blasts of the ship's whistle—a distress signal—at regular intervals. Meanwhile, the ship's radio operator, Lorenz Connelly, sent repeated distress calls to the Coast Guard in Boston. He also tried to signal the Portland Lightship with a flashing light but got no response. Suddenly, two lights appeared through the storm from the direction of the

The *Oakey L. Alexander* on the rocks at Cape Elizabeth on March 3, 1947.
Courtesy of the Museum at Portland Head Light.

shore, one fixed and one flashing. They were the two lighthouses at
Cape Elizabeth.

Captain Lewis ordered the engines slowed as he tried to aim the
ship for Crescent Beach, west of the light station. "She rode the sea
to the ledges much like a surfboard," he said later. The men braced
themselves for impact and the ship crashed onto the rocks about
150 yards offshore from McKenney Point, between Crescent Beach
and the Cape Elizabeth lighthouses and Coast Guard Station. It was
six-fifteen in the morning when the ship came to rest, moderately
listing to port.

At the Coast Guard lifesaving station adjacent to the lighthouses,
the men on duty had first heard the blasts from the *Alexander* shortly
after four-thirty. The seas were too rough to launch a lifeboat, so the
Coast Guardsmen readied equipment that included a Lyle gun. The
officer in charge, Earle Drinkwater, took his six-man crew to the
point of land nearest the *Alexander,* which they found by following
the sound of the whistle blasts. Several local fishermen and Coast
Guard veterans, as well as some men from the Coast Guard station
in South Portland, eventually joined the Coast Guardsmen, whose

The thirty-two men aboard the *Oakey L. Alexander* were all
brought ashore safely via breeches buoy.
Courtesy of the Museum at Portland Head Light.

crew had been reduced in number from eleven because of budget
cuts.

It was shortly after eight o'clock that morning by the time the
men were ready to fire the Lyle gun. The small, short-barreled cannon, used to fire a line to vessels in distress, was rarely employed
anymore. It could throw a line up to three hundred yards on a full
charge. For many years it was customary for lifesaving crews—or
surfmen, as they were called—to practice the breeches buoy drill
every Thursday afternoon. The Lyle gun and all associated equipment had to be maintained in pristine condition.

"The only time I ever saw one of those Lyle guns," Drinkwater
said later, "was during training drills with the Coast Guard." After
the gun was positioned on a ledge, Drinkwater carefully loaded
the eighteen-pound shot. He positioned the faking box, which
held hundreds of feet of strong linen rope attached to the shot. He
rubbed the first few feet of the line in the mud so it wouldn't be
burned when the gun was fired.

Calling to everyone around him to stand back, Drinkwater
fired the gun. His first shot was right on target. "It was more good

judgment than luck," he said later. "If it had been luck, it would have been because I closed my eyes and let her go, but it was darn good judgment, considering the wind."

The men on the *Alexander* secured the shot, which had a spindle and eye on its end, to the highest and safest spot they could reach on the ship. Drinkwater sent across a pulley, known as a tail block, threaded with a looped or "endless" line called a whip. The tail block was firmly secured aboard the *Alexander*. The tail block and whip were then used to send a strong, three-inch hawser across to the ship, and the hawser was secured. Finally, the breeches buoy—a kind of canvas sling attached to a ring resembling a life preserver, with two openings for the legs to go through—was sent across.

The hawser was threaded through a "traveling block," from which the breeches buoy was suspended with four strong lines. The traveling block was also fastened to the whip.

When everything was ready, Drinkwater shouted to the men on the *Alexander,* "Who wants to go first?" The eighteen-year-old mess boy, David Rogers—the youngest on the crew—volunteered. He climbed into the breeches buoy and made the ride to shore in about five minutes. He was struck by the high surf several times on the way across, and he later confessed, "I got nervous until I had reached the shore. When I looked back at the ship and the surf, I lost my nerve."

When he arrived, Rogers informed the lifesavers that all hands aboard the *Alexander* were safe. The rest of the men on the collier rode safely, one at a time, to shore. "We had very good luck," said Drinkwater. "The toughest part was battling the wind squalls which threatened to dunk the men as they rode the buoy. As it was, only three of the thirty-two were dunked."

A local observer later recalled, "It was strange to see each crew member as he swung back and forth like a bag of clothes on a line." There was a nerve-racking moment when the radio operator, Lorenz Connelly, was partway across. The lines jammed, and Connelly was dunked into the waves for about twenty seconds. He was rushed to the hospital and soon recovered.

The first mate, John Walker, was the next to last to arrive on

Captain Raymond Lewis of the *Oakey L. Alexander.* Courtesy of the Museum at Portland Head Light.

shore. At that point Captain Lewis sent a message to shore that he would remain on the vessel to protect the owner's interests. He was assured that a security watch would be posted, and he left the ship.

Captain Lewis reflected on the hundreds of eventless voyages he had made on the *Alexander,* then climbed into the breeches buoy and made the five-minute ride to shore, where he was greeted by cheers. In the first message Lewis sent to the manager of the Pocahontas Steamship Company, he wrote, "Crew are to be commended for their calm and collected conduct. Every man did his part and well."

Lewis, who had performed heroically by all measures, told the press, "The Coast Guard men did it. Those fellows were right on the button." Lewis was praised, in turn, by the Coast Guard for "showing the highest degree of seamanship in saving the lives of his entire crew."

At nine o'clock that morning, as the men were being rescued from the *Alexander,* a few miles away at Portland Head Lighthouse, two tremendous waves in succession shattered a sixteen-inch-thick brick wall of the fog signal building and knocked a fog bell from its stand into a gully. "I don't think I'll ever witness another such double wave in my life!" Keeper William L. Lockhart told the historian Edward Rowe Snow.

Another collier was soon christened *Oakey L. Alexander.* It was a converted 439-foot Liberty ship that had been bought by the Pocahontas Steamship Company. The second *Alexander*'s first captain was Raymond Lewis.

Edward Rowe Snow, who lived in Massachusetts, hurried to Maine on the day of the *Alexander* rescue. He interviewed Earle Drinkwater and asked if there was anything he'd like to have mentioned.

"Why, yes," Drinkwater replied. "It would be fine if you'd mention my men: Robbins, Taylor, Spaulding, Doucette, Brown, and Morong, and the men from the South Portland Base. Then there were the fishermen, and the retired Coast Guardsmen, who came when they were needed. You should mention Roscoe Dennison, Verne Reynolds, and Melcher Beal. They deserve the praise of everyone who hears about it. I'd like to thank them all."

The bow section of the *Oakey L. Alexander* was never found. Countless sightseers viewed the wrecked *Alexander*, just offshore at Cape Elizabeth. One enterprising local restaurateur set up a food stand nearby to cater to the throngs of tourists.

Salvage crews recovered about a thousand tons of coal, along with some parts of the hull and superstructure. According to the book *New England's Legacy of Shipwrecks,* by Henry Keats, artifacts are still recovered from the wreck, especially after storms. "The wreck is always talking—moaning and groaning," Keats wrote. "The surge moves metal plates, producing sounds that can be bewildering to a diver." Some of the remains of the *Alexander* can still be seen from boats at low tide.

CHAPTER TEN

More Wrecks along the Maine Coast

FOLLOWING ARE accounts of more of Maine's notable wrecks and rescues, in chronological order.

ONE OF THE best-known early shipwrecks often attributed to the Maine coast was that of the *Grand Design,* carrying two hundred Irish immigrants in 1741. According to most sources, the ship went aground at Mount Desert Island. Most of the passengers died in the months that followed, until help arrived after some local Indians paddled many miles to take letters from the survivors to the town of St. George, Maine.

It's a story of tragedy and survival that's been told and retold through the centuries. As it turns out, it's usually been told with most of the basic facts wrong. Recent research by Julia Lane of Round Pond, Maine, has revealed that the true name of the ship was the *Martha and Eliza,* and it was wrecked not on the Maine coast but on Grand Manan Island, New Brunswick, Canada. Because it did not occur on the Maine coast, no further details will be included here.

THE EAST INDIAMAN *Grand Turk,* built in Salem, Massachusetts, in 1791, returned to Portland after a long trade voyage to China on December 28, 1797. As the officers from the ship enjoyed a dance in their honor at a Portland hall, a storm arrived in Portland Harbor. Drifting ice severed the anchor cables of the *Grand Turk,* and it ran aground at Stanford's Ledge.

The *Grand Turk*'s guns and some other items were thrown

overboard in an effort to refloat the ship, but the storm forced the ship into the rocks at Cushing's Point, and it was a total loss. Some of the treasures aboard, including Chinese porcelain and silk, were salvaged, but much of the cargo found its way into the homes of Cape Elizabeth citizens. "Finery from the *Grand Turk*," wrote the Cape Elizabeth historian William B. Jordan Jr., "added a note of unaccustomed luxury to many a humble home at the Cape for years to come."

THE FIRST RECORDED shipwreck near Cape Elizabeth involving loss of life was that of the schooner *Charles,* which ran onto a ledge in thick fog late in the night of July 12, 1807. There were twenty-two people (or twenty-three, according to some accounts) on board the packet schooner, which traveled between Portland and Boston. The captain, Jacob Adams, swam to shore, but drowned when he returned to the vessel in a desperate attempt to save his wife, who also drowned. Only six people survived.

One of the victims of the *Charles* disaster, twenty-four-year-old Lydia Carver of Freeport, was returning from a visit to Boston to purchase her wedding dress. Her body was found on the beach next to a trunk containing the dress. Local legend claims that her spirit is seen walking the beach, dressed in white.

Lydia Carver is buried in a small cemetery near Crescent Beach in the town of Cape Elizabeth, near what is now the Inn by the Sea. A local man, Jack Coggeshall, was using the inn's pool with some friends a few years ago when they saw something unusual—a woman wearing a light gown flowing in the wind, about fifty yards away. "It had a funny glow to it. She was watching us," Coggeshall told a reporter, "and we stared back. Then I turned away, and when I looked back again, she was gone."

THE BORDER BETWEEN the states of New Hampshire and Maine runs virtually through the middle of the Isles of Shoals, a rocky archipelago several miles off the New Hampshire seacoast. The islands' colorful history includes legends of pirates and ghosts and, of course, shipwrecks. Many sources describe the wreck of a Spanish ship called the *Sagunto* on Smuttynose Island, which belongs to Maine, in a January 1813 snowstorm. Thirteen to sixteen men died in the wreck, according to different versions, and were buried on the island.

Celia Thaxter, the poet and author who spent her life on the Isles of Shoals, popularized the shipwreck in her poem "The Spaniards' Graves":

> O sailors, did sweet eyes look after you
> The day you sailed away from sunny Spain?
> Bright eyes that followed fading ship and crew,
> Melting in tender rain? . . .
>
> Spanish women, over the far seas,
> Could I but show you where your dead repose!
> Could I send tidings on this northern breeze
> That strong and steady blows!

According to Thaxter's book *Among the Isles of Shoals* and other sources, Captain Sam Haley buried the sailors. The New Hampshire seacoast historian and author J. Dennis Robinson has researched the story, and he points out that Haley had died two years earlier, in 1811, at the age of eighty. It is possible, however, that his son, also known as Captain Haley, found the bodies. Lyman Rutledge, in his book *The Isles of Shoals in Lore and Legend,* wrote that the wrecked ship was not the *Sagunto,* which had arrived in Newport from Cádiz, Spain, two days earlier, but the *Concepción,* also from Cádiz.

Samuel Adams Drake wrote in *A Book of New England Legends and Folklore* that the account of the shipwreck in the Gosport town records (the Isles of Shoals once made up the town of Gosport) is in error, as the *Sagunto* made port safely. But he did believe that a large Spanish or Portuguese vessel was wrecked on the ledges at Smuttynose.

The historian Edward Rowe Snow, while recovering from war wounds in a hospital in Oran, North Africa, in 1942, met a Spanish woman who claimed that some of her ancestors had been aboard a doomed ship that was lost in New England in 1813.

Archaeological digs on the island have failed to clear up the mysteries of the Smuttynose wreck. Robinson points out that the topsoil on the stony island is only about a foot deep, making it unlikely that anyone was buried there. "So for now," Robinson writes, "we're left with a sinking ship of facts, a conflicting sea of words, some piles of rocks, a storm of misplaced emotions."

THE *Dash* was a topsail schooner built in Freeport by the Porter brothers, Portland merchants, in 1813. On one of its first voyages, the *Dash* went to Santo Domingo and returned to Portland with a cargo of coffee. This was during the War of 1812, and a British man-of-war fired at the *Dash* on the return voyage. The schooner was much too fast for its pursuer, and there was no damage except a broken foremast. The *Dash* was then outfitted as a brig.

Later in the war, the *Dash* began a new career as a privateer. It was so successful in that role, taking many British ships and cargoes, that the captain won an appointment as the customs inspector at Portland.

Under the leadership of a new captain, twenty-four-year-old John Porter—a brother of the ship's builders—the *Dash* continued its highly successful privateering. In January 1815 the crew was unaware that a treaty had been signed that ended hostilities, and they were eager to get back to sea. The *Dash* left Portland Harbor alongside the privateer *Champlain,* as Porter had accepted a challenge for a race.

As the two ships sailed out to sea, the *Dash* was well in the lead for more than twenty-four hours. A snowstorm was sweeping into the region, and the *Dash* sailed right into the teeth of the storm, while the *Champlain* was able to return to the harbor safely.

The *Dash* and its crew (the number of men was anywhere from thirty-seven to sixty) were never seen again. Captain Porter left a young wife, whom he had wed only months before. It's believed the *Dash* met its end on Georges Bank, always treacherous in rough weather. Seward Porter, who lost three brothers in the disaster, lobbied for a lighthouse on the bank, with no success.

Over the years, legend has it, the phantom ship *Dash* has been seen by fishermen and boaters, and even by people onshore. One version of the story claims that every time a family member of a *Dash* crewman died, the ghost ship appeared to bear the loved one on his or her final journey. It's said that during World War II, the crews of U.S. Navy ships in Casco Bay observed the *Dash* sailing through the fog, bound for home.

WHALEBACK LEDGE, off Kittery, Maine, marks the entrance to the Piscataqua River and the harbor of Portsmouth, New Hampshire. A lighthouse was established on the ledge in 1830. Before the lighthouse was erected, ships struck the ledge with sickening regularity. In April 1821 the schooner *President,* heading to Thomaston, Maine, from Boston, struck Whaleback Ledge. The vessel and its cargo were a complete loss.

As the crew and passengers struggled in the waves, several boats full of soldiers arrived from Fort Constitution in New Castle, New Hampshire, about a mile away. Most of the would-be rescuers opted not to get too close to the ledges in the heavy seas. According to a newspaper account, Corporal George McAuley asked his crew, "Shall we save them or perish in the attempt?" The response was unanimously "Yes," and seven people from the wrecked vessel were soon saved from certain death.

IN HIS BOOK *Great Storms and Famous Shipwrecks of the New England Coast,* Edward Rowe Snow told the tale of the packet *Sarah,* which was sailing from Boston to Eastport, Maine, in 1835. The captain confused Mount Desert Rock Lighthouse with Moose Peak Lighthouse, some fifty miles to the northeast. As a result, the ship was wrecked on a ledge near Jonesport.

Sixteen people died in the wreck, but a woman passenger swam safely to shore with a boy, Daniel Goulden, clinging to her. A ballad was published soon after the wreck, "The Loss of the *Sarah,*" which reads in part:

> Ye landsmen all, now pray draw near,
> A lamentation ye shall hear;
> A ship was lost on the sea,
> It was the *Sarah*'s lot to be.

Thirty and two were the *Sarah's* crew
And landsmen were all counted too;
Sixteen survived to reach the shore,
Sixteen are lost, they are no more.

LIKE SO MANY maritime regions around the world, the southern Maine coast has its ghost ship legend. On October 13, 1842, the new bark *Isidore* (or *Isadore*) left Kennebunk with a crew of fifteen men (the number differs slightly in various accounts), bound for New Orleans with a cargo of hay and potatoes. The vessel was owned by several local shipmasters, including the captain, Leander Foss. The entire crew was made up of local young men from Kennebunk.

The previous night one of the crew, Thomas King, had had a series of dreams that he later related in a letter:

In the first place I dreamed I was on board the bark, going down Kennebunk river, and when we got to the piers every person in the bark disappeared. And I sang out "Good Lord, what has brought me on board this bark all sole alone." At this outcry my wife woke me. And I went to sleep again and the same dream was repeated. My wife woke me the second time. Again I slept and the same dream was repeated the same as in the two preceding instances, only I was not disturbed again by my wife, as in the two previous dreams. I looked on deck and I saw eighteen empty coffins and made inquiries what they were for. In answer to my question Capt. Foss said there was one a piece for each of the crew, but I was so poor there was none for me, by this time the bark had got out some way and she was laboring heavy and on her beam ends and her maintop gallant sail had got adrift and the Capt. wanted to know if he had a man on board that would go and save the sail. I made this reply that I was not afraid to go to any part of the bark as long as the spar and rigging would hold. And I went and saved it. And I looked from the yardarm into the water and I saw a large flat rock and I leaped from the yardarm on to it. But instead of leaping to the rock I had leaped over my wife and child and again my wife woke me and I found I was standing

89

on the floor. It made an impression on my mind that something would happen to the vessel and no threats or persuasion could induce me to go to sea in her.

King was so shaken that he hid in the woods nearby, where the captain and other crewmen couldn't find him. Another sailor also had a premonition of doom. Tragically, he didn't heed the warning.

Not long after leaving Kennebunk, the *Isidore* ran into a blinding snowstorm. The ship crashed into the rocks at Bald Head Cliffs in York, and all the men aboard were lost in the icy waves. On the same night, six passengers died when the schooner *James Clark* was wrecked at Rye, New Hampshire.

It's been claimed that the *Isidore* sometimes appears as a phantom ship, sailing slowly along the southern Maine coast. Sometimes the ghostly crew is seen on board, staring straight ahead. When another vessel comes close to offer assistance, the *Isidore* vanishes into thin air.

DAVID SPINNEY was the keeper at Pond Island Lighthouse, off the mouth of the Kennebec River, on November 10, 1849, when the ship *Hanover,* returning to Bath from Cádiz with a cargo of Spanish salt, anchored near the island in a storm. As the storm raged, the captain tried to tack around the island and enter the western passage into the river. The ship ran into a bar off nearby Wood Island and soon sank with all twenty-four crewmen on board. Only a dog survived.

Milton Spinney, son of the lighthouse keeper, wrote an eyewitness account of the disaster:

> Taking the western way was one of the many unexplainable things connected with this tragedy. After lying all the forenoon in a position where he could easily have entered the river, Captain Rogers was seen to square away his yard, run down to leeward of Seguin and try to get in the western way.
>
> Then we saw from our lookout that the Captain was going to put his ship about. Slowly the vessel came up to wind, but a short distance from the seething foam of the bar and dead to windward of it.

When in the wind's eye she refused to go farther and with all her sails aback she slowly forged astern. Back, back, until every watcher's heart was ready to burst with suspense, back to that fearful maelstrom. Back, to the octopus whose arms were extended to receive the doomed ship and her crew. Back, till in the hollow of a huge wave her stempost struck the sand beneath and the story is told.

The ship, when she struck, fell off broadside to the sea and the next comber rolled her down on her broadside, then every man on board, twenty-four all told, were seen on her side. The next waves rolled her bottom-up, breaking her spars off. As she rolled over the crew clambered up over the bilge and strung themselves out, holding on to the keel.

The third and fourth seas broke the ship in pieces and left the crew to battle for their lives till death should end their troubles. We knew that no man could come through alive.

As the wreckage came floating ashore the men went on the beach, and as the bodies came ashore they were reverently carried up on the high ground and laid down. Before the end of the day the bodies had been secured and now lie buried in a little cemetery within sound of the roaring waves which beat them to death.

When the body of Captain George Rogers was recovered, it was apparent that he had prepared himself to go ashore at his home port by shaving and donning his best suit. The Maine Maritime Museum in Bath has in its collection three baskets that washed ashore from the *Hanover,* as well as a sequence of four paintings depicting the tragic shipwreck.

DURING A FIERCE snowstorm that swept the Maine coast on December 22, 1850, five vessels went aground between Rockland Harbor and Spruce Head. The schooner *Niagara* dragged anchor and struck a ledge; the crew was evacuated safely.

A small schooner from Massachusetts anchored during the early part of the storm at Jameson's Point, on the north side of the entrance to Rockland Harbor. The captain went ashore, leaving the mate, Richard B. Ingraham, a seaman named Roger Elliott, and one passenger, Lydia Dyer, who was engaged to Ingraham. The packet was to start for Boston the next morning.

Near midnight the storm intensified. The schooner parted anchor and careened to the other side of the harbor, where it smashed into the rocky ledges south of the Owls Head Lighthouse. The three on board huddled together on the deck and were soon virtually frozen in the surf. They pulled blankets around themselves in an effort to stay dry.

As the schooner broke apart, Elliott escaped the vessel and clambered over the ice-covered rocks to the shore. Practically dead from exhaustion, he reached the road to the lighthouse. The keeper happened to be driving by in a sleigh, and he took the dazed Elliott to the light station, where he gave him hot rum and put him in bed.

Barely capable of speech, Elliott was able to tell the keeper about the others still on the schooner. A dozen men were rounded up, and they headed for the shore. The rescue party soon found the schooner and went on board. There they found a block of ice enveloping Ingraham and Dyer. From all appearances the couple was dead, but the rescue party was determined to leave nothing to chance.

The men took the block to the kitchen of the keeper's house. They chipped the ice away, keeping the pair in cold water. Then they slowly raised the temperature of the water and began to exercise the limbs of the victims. After almost two hours of massaging and exercising, Lydia Dyer showed signs of life. An hour later Ingraham opened his eyes and said, "What is all this? Where are we?"

By the next day Dyer and Ingraham were able to eat, but it was months before they recovered. They eventually married and had four children. Roger Elliott never fully recovered, but his struggle to reach safety had resulted in the rescue of the other two. Lydia Dyer and Richard Ingraham will always be celebrated as the "Frozen Couple of Owls Head."

THE ESTABLISHMENT OF a lighthouse in 1830 at Whaleback Ledge, at the mouth of the Piscataqua River near Kittery, did much to protect shipping, but it couldn't put an end to shipwrecks. In the early hours of February 15, 1863, the British schooner *Rouser,* on its way to Boston from St. John, New Brunswick, was wrecked close to the ledge. It was reported that the lighthouse keeper, Joel P. Reynolds, looked out the window of the tower at five o'clock in the morning and saw a piece of the wreck, along with three men. One of the men called to the keeper, pleading for him to throw them a line. The keeper immediately complied, but the seas were too rough for the men to be saved. All seven men on board the *Rouser* died in the tragedy. Soon after the wreck, a new fog bell was installed at the lighthouse.

A POWERFUL STORM ON September 8, 1869, drove the Glouces-ter schooner *Helen Eliza,* which had anchored off Peaks Island near Portland, into the rocks. Only one of the twelve men aboard reached the island alive. Ten bodies, including that of Captain Charles Jor-dan, were later recovered.

A LIGHTHOUSE KEEPER, Marcus Aurelius Hanna, was responsible for one of Maine's most celebrated maritime rescues. On the night of January 28, 1885, Hanna was suffering from a bad cold at the Cape Elizabeth Light Station. A storm hit and increased in severity as the night progressed. Hanna sounded the steam fog whistle all night despite being ill and exhausted. Hiram Staples, the assistant keeper, relieved Hanna at six the next morning. The blizzard was by then "one of the coldest and most violent storms of snow, wind and vapor . . . that I ever witnessed," Hanna later said. He had to crawl through enormous snowdrifts back to the house. The temperature was 4 degrees below zero.

Hanna was soon asleep. His wife, Louise (Davis), who held one of the assistant keeper positions for some years, extinguished the lights in both towers after sunrise. Not long after, at eight-forty, she looked out toward the ocean and saw a schooner aground on Dyer's Ledge, near the fog signal building.

The vessel was the *Australia* out of Boothbay, which had been headed for Boston with a cargo of ice from the Kennebec River in the hold and 150 barrels of mackerel on deck. The captain had already been swept away by the waves; only two crewmen remained alive. The men had climbed to the rigging and were practically frozen alive in the bitter cold.

Louise Hanna shouted to her husband, informing him that a vessel was ashore. The keeper rushed to the signal house. Staples hadn't seen the wreck through the thick snow. The two men hurried to the edge of the water near the schooner. Hanna later recalled, "I felt a terrible responsibility thrust upon me, and I resolved to attempt the rescue at any hazard." He tried a number of times to throw a line to the vessel but failed. Staples returned to the fog signal building. Meanwhile, Hanna's wife alerted neighbors.

Hanna, himself nearly frozen by this time, waded waist-deep into the ocean and again threw a line to the schooner, this time hitting his target. One of the crewmen, Irving Pierce, managed to pull himself from the rigging and tied the line around him. Hanna somehow pulled the helpless man through the waves and over the

Ram Island Ledge Lighthouse was built in 1905 at a dangerous obstruction on the approach to Portland Harbor. U.S. Coast Guard photo.

rocks to the shore. According to Hanna, "Pierce's jaws were set; he was totally blind from exposure to the cold, and the expression of his face I shall not soon forget."

After several tries, Hanna landed the line on the *Australia* again. The other crewman, William Kellar, tied the rope around himself. Hanna's strength was giving out and he faltered as he tried to pull the man to safety. Just then, Staples and two neighbors arrived. The four men hauled Kellar to the shore, and then carried the two sailors to the fog signal building. The men were given dry clothes and, once they had thawed enough, hot food and drink. After two days they had recovered enough to be taken to Portland by sled.

Six months later Marcus Hanna received a gold lifesaving medal for "heroism involving great peril to his life," in recognition of one of the greatest lifesaving feats at an American lighthouse. In August 1997 the Coast Guard launched a new $12.5 million 175-foot buoy tender named the *Marcus Hanna*. A replica of Hanna's lifesaving medal is mounted on board. The cutter's home port is South Portland, Maine.

DANGEROUS LEDGES surround Ram Island, on the easterly approach to Portland Harbor. Shipwrecks occurred there with frequency; local tradition held that the ledge, aptly described as a "jagged disarray of hungry monsters" by the historian Herbert Milton Sylvester, claimed a vessel every seven years.

On May 27, 1866, alone there were four wrecks. Many fishing boats and schooners struck the ledges over the years, often while trying to make Portland Harbor in bad weather. On February 24, 1900, the four-hundred-foot transatlantic Allan Line steamer *Californian*, bound for England from Portland with a crew of ninety-six and twenty-one passengers, along with $300,000 in freight, went aground at the outer end of the ledge in a snowstorm. There was no loss of life, and the steamer was refloated six weeks later. This near tragedy finally convinced the federal government that a lighthouse was called for, and Congress appropriated the needed funds in 1902–3.

The schooner *Glenrosa*, carrying a cargo of coal, struck the ledge on September 20, 1902, and was a total loss, but its crew of eight survived. Then, on December 8, the fishing vessel *Cora and Lillian* ran into the east side of the ledge with a full cargo of fish. The crew managed to get safely ashore at Portland Head.

In the predawn hours of January 12, 1905, just a few months before the lighthouse went into service, the *Leona,* a schooner heading from Rockland, Maine, to Rockport, Massachusetts, with a cargo of lime, struck near Ram Island in a snowstorm. The captain and four crewmen launched a lifeboat and managed to stay afloat for a few hours, until the construction workers at the ledge saw one of their flares. The workers directed the lifeboat to a cove near the lighthouse and then helped the nearly frozen men get safely ashore.

On December 9, 1902, an assistant keeper on night duty at Mount Desert Rock Light Station, more than twenty miles offshore from Mount Desert Island, heard several blasts from a boat's whistle. It wasn't until daybreak and low tide that Fred Robbins, the principal keeper, and his assistant were able to ascertain that a boat was on the rocks at the end of the island known as Northeast Point.

The disabled boat was the New York tug *Astral.* With a barge in tow, it had run aground with a crew of eighteen men aboard. By the time the keepers reached the scene, one young crewman had already frozen to death. After several tries, Robbins and the assistant managed to get close enough to the vessel to get a line aboard. Robbins said later that it was "with the superhuman strength of absolute desperation" that they were able to haul the men to safety.

The *Astral* rolled over and sank just minutes after the men were rescued. Meanwhile, several men on board the barge that was being towed by the *Astral* hoisted sail and made it all the way to Rockland.

The keeper's wife, Lillie Robbins, prepared plenty of steaming coffee for the survivors, and salve from the station's medicine chest was applied to the men's freezing limbs. Many of the men had lost flesh from their hands and had to be spoon-fed. The crew remained at the station until the storm subsided six days later, and Lillie Robbins kept them well fed. The seas were still rough when the Boston tug *Clara Clarita* arrived to take the men off the Rock.

Early 1900s view of the Cape Elizabeth Lifesaving Station.
From the collection of the author.

In *A History of Cape Elizabeth, Maine,* William B. Jordan Jr. wrote
that there had been, as of 1964, eighty-one known vessels totaling
approximately 23,000 tons of shipping lost in the vicinity of Cape
Elizabeth. The crews at the Cape Elizabeth Lifesaving Station, which
was in operation at Dyer's Cove from 1887 to 1964, rescued the crews
and passengers in many of these incidents.

One of the more notable rescues by the Cape Elizabeth crew
occurred on June 12, 1903, when the spectacular five-masted schooner *Washington B. Thomas,* built in Thomaston, Maine, was bound
for Portland with four thousand tons of coal in heavy weather. The
crew anchored the vessel in Saco Bay to ride out the storm, but the
anchor dragged and the 2,639-ton schooner ran onto a reef near
Stratton Island, off Prout's Neck.

The lifesaving crew was alerted and soon arrived on the scene.
To reach the *Thomas* the crew had to use four horses to haul their
surfboat to Prout's Neck. The men reached the schooner in the
churning seas and rescued the captain, William J. Lermond, and
most of his crew. The captain's young wife, Hattie May (Winchen-
bach), had already been pulled from her husband's arms by the high
seas and drowned before the lifesavers arrived.

The rescue took several hours. Bowdoin Lermond, the sixteen-year-old son of the captain, clung to the wreck for five hours before he was saved. The *Thomas* had been launched only two months before the wreck.

ON SEPTEMBER 16, 1903, while Clarence Marr was the keeper at Pemaquid Point Lighthouse, the captain of the Gloucester fishing schooner *George F. Edmunds* tried to run for South Bristol Harbor in a gale. The vessel was driven by a strong gust into the rocks near Pemaquid Point and dashed to pieces. The captain and thirteen crewmen died in the wreck; only two were saved.

Another schooner, the *Sadie and Lillie,* went aground at Pemaquid Point in the same storm. A local man, Weston Curtis, was able to get a line to the two-masted vessel, and two crewmen were helped safely to shore. The captain, William S. Harding, made it about halfway to shore, but was drowned in the heavy seas as his would-be rescuers tried desperately to save him.

THE FOUR-MASTED, 227-foot schooner *Alice B. Clark,* built in Bath and based in Portland, struck a ledge in Penobscot Bay near Islesboro in stormy, foggy weather on July 1, 1909. The crew of eight escaped, but the cargo of coal was lost.

ON DECEMBER 9, 1915, the crew of the sloop *Flora D. Thompson* anchored near Seguin Island, waiting for the right moment to continue into the Kennebec River. There were seven people on board, including four women and children. Strong winds developed that night and the *Thompson* parted its cable and drifted out to sea. The keeper of the Hunnewell's (Hunniwell's) Beach Lifesaving Station observed the *Thompson,* and in the morning a lifesaving crew headed out in a power surfboat.

On the way to the *Thompson,* the lifesavers came alongside the new destroyer *Conyngham,* which was engaged in a trial run. The lifesavers enlisted the help of the destroyer, knowing that their small boat wouldn't be sufficient to tow in the *Thompson* if that should be necessary.

When the two vessels reached the *Thompson,* it was laboring badly. A cookstove had been thrown overboard and was serving as a makeshift anchor. The destroyer proceeded to tow both boats toward shore. All went well until they reached the vicinity of Seguin Island, when the rough seas began to break the *Thompson* apart. The seven aboard the *Thompson* were swiftly taken aboard the surfboat. They were subsequently put safely aboard the tug *Cumberland,* which had just arrived on the scene. The *Cumberland* finished the job of towing both boats to the lifesaving station wharf. According to a Coast Guard report, the rescued persons were suffering from "fright and exposure," and they were given "restorative attention" at the station.

Just a few days later, on the night of December 13, 1915, surfmen at the Hunnewell's Beach Lifesaving Station noticed the schooner *Irene E. Messervey* in a dangerous position near Seguin Island in heavy seas. Shortly after dawn, a crew tried to set out in a surfboat to reach the schooner, but the conditions were too rough and they had to turn back.

Later in the morning, the cutter *Ossipee* pulled up close to the schooner and shot a hawser aboard, but the crew of the *Messervey* was unable to secure the line. Finally, about noon, a line was gotten aboard the schooner and it was towed to safety. The captain had been severely injured and was taken to a hospital for immediate surgery.

THE 281-FOOT passenger steamer *Bay State,* built in 1895, was a sister ship to the ill-fated *Portland,* which was lost in a monumental storm in Massachusetts Bay in November 1898. In the predawn hours of September 23, 1916, the *Bay State* ran aground at McKenney Point on Cape Elizabeth, close to the spot where the *Oakey L. Alexander* would be stranded more than thirty years later. The men at the Cape Elizabeth Lifesaving Station safely evacuated the passengers and crew, 250 people in all.

The huge steamer remained just offshore for months and was seen by many residents and tourists. It's said that a number of homes in the vicinity were paneled with woodwork from the *Bay State,* and some took their carpeting from the staterooms. The ship eventually broke apart in a storm.

CLARENCE MARR was still the keeper at Pemaquid Point on August 17, 1917, when the schooner *Willis and Guy* struck the rocks near the lighthouse in heavy fog. The crew escaped safely, but the vessel was destroyed and its cargo of coal was scattered four days later when a hurricane swept the coast. Local residents gathered the coal and saved on heating costs that winter.

A DOUBLE SHIPWRECK near Goat Island, off Cape Porpoise, on January 1–2, 1920, would not be particularly noteworthy except for the fact that the wrecks of the two three-masted schooners occurred close to the lighthouse on Goat Island. Several photographers immortalized the unusual occurrence.

First, the *Charles H. Trickey,* carrying boxboard from Portland to Lynn, Massachusetts, ran aground near midnight on New Year's Day when the crew tried to take it on the wrong side of a spindle in rough seas. A short time later, in the early morning hours of January 2, the *Mary E. Olys,* carrying granite from Stonington, Maine, to Ossining, New York, ran onto a ledge in an attempt to pass on the starboard side of the *Trickey.* The four-man crews of both vessels escaped without injury with the help of the cutter *Ossipee.* The cargoes were unloaded, but the schooners were a total loss.

THE 250-FOOT-LONG freighter *Polias* was constructed of concrete at the Fougner Shipbuilding Company in Flushing, New York, at a cost of more than $2 million. The *Polias* was the first commissioned ship in the United States Emergency Fleet, which was intended to be a merchant fleet for the U.S. government during World War I. President Woodrow Wilson had approved the construction of twenty-four concrete ships because of the short supply of steel. Only twelve of them were actually built, and none of them was put in service before the war had ended.

The *Polias* was launched in January 1919. Beginning in late 1919 it was used to transport coal for the New York and Porto

The double wreck off Goat Island in January 1920. From the collection of Edward Rowe Snow, courtesy of Dorothy Bicknell.

Rico Steamship Company. Just a few months later, during a severe cold snap in February 1920, the ship was headed to Norfolk, Virginia, after unloading a cargo of coal at Searsport, Maine. It was the *Polias*'s fifth voyage, and thirty-eight men were aboard, including Captain Richard T. Coughlan. They encountered extensive ice floes as the ship passed through West Penobscot Bay during a severe snowstorm.

Early on the evening of February 6, the freighter struck Old Cilley Ledge, about five miles south of Port Clyde. The forward section suffered severe damage, and the ship grounded soon after impact. Messages of distress were quickly sent, but the men didn't know how long the damaged ship could withstand the heavy seas that crashed against the hull.

As they waited for help to arrive, the captain warned the crew not to attempt an escape with the lifeboats. Against his orders, eleven crewmen lowered one of the boats into the dark, turbulent water, and pulled away. They were never seen again.

Lifesaving crews arrived the next day and the rest of the men were safely removed from the *Polias*. The ship couldn't be saved, but it remained mostly intact until a hurricane in 1924 rolled it over and broke it apart. At low tide, some of the remains can still be seen in about thirty feet of water.

ON THE FOGGY MORNING of March 9, 1921, the 3,991-ton British steam freighter *Wandby,* coming from Algiers and headed for Portland, was off Kennebunkport. The captain, David Simpson, thought the ship was much closer to Portland than it actually was; he had mistaken a whistling buoy off Cape Porpoise for a buoy on Cash's Ledge, southeast of the Portland Lightship. Just after Simpson left the bridge, the lookout shouted, "Breakers ahead!" The captain ordered the assistant engineer, William D. Gilbertson, to turn full astern. As he did so, there was a terrific grinding and the captain ordered the engines stopped. The ship came to a halt only about sixty feet from shore, a thirty-foot gash in the bow.

A caretaker at the George H. Walker estate in Kennebunkport who witnessed the accident later said that the sound of the great ship going aground was "strongly suggestive of a boiler factory falling down two flights of stairs." Local residents hurried to the scene. An artist, Louis Norton, brought his pastels, thinking there might be something good to draw. There was so much excitement in town that schools closed early so that the children could watch the effort to move the freighter off the rocks.

At first the crew of the Coast Guard cutter *Ossipee* was unable to see the *Wandby* because of thick fog. The weather began to clear by mid-afternoon, but efforts to refloat the ship were abandoned when high tide flooded the engine room. The crew all escaped safely. For the next three weeks the captain and crewmen stayed in the vicinity, taking part in dances, digging clams, and selling Scotch whiskey from the *Wandby* to Kennebunkport residents for five dollars a bottle.

Captain Simpson was demoted to first mate on another ship owned by the same company, but he made it back to captain within two years. The wreck was later sold for scrap and most of it was removed, but pieces of the *Wandby*'s hull remain near Walker's Point, the summer home of George H. W. and Barbara Bush. One of the guest cottages at the estate is named *Wandby* in commemoration of the shipwreck.

THE PASSENGER STEAMER *City of Rockland*, built in Boston in 1900, had a troubled career marked by several collisions and groundings. In 1904 the 274-foot vessel, which was capable of carrying two thousand passengers, struck a ledge in Maine's Muscle Ridge Channel in thick fog. After it was repaired in Boston, the steamer's next misadventure was a 1906 collision with its sister ship, the *City of Bangor.*

Then, on September 2, 1923, the steamer ran aground in thick fog with three hundred passengers at Dix's Island in the Kennebec River, near Parker's Head, a half hour after leaving Bath en route to Boston. Surfboats from the Popham Beach Lifesaving Station soon arrived, and everyone was removed safely. The passengers huddled around a bonfire onshore at Popham Beach and were supplied with blankets and food from the steamer.

According to Edward Rowe Snow, "The children, while sliding

The steamer *City of Rockland* went aground at Dix's Island, on the Kennebec River, in 1923. From the collection of the author.

down the sloping sides of the steamer into the boats, enlivened the proceedings by their songs, singing at the top of their voices, *Yes, We Have No Bananas,* and *Barney Google,* the favorites of the period." The passengers were returned to Bath, where they boarded a train for Boston. The *City of Rockland* was taken to Salem, Massachusetts, where everything usable was removed, and what was left was burned at Little Misery Island.

THE DANGEROUS ROCKS near West Quoddy Head in Lubec, at the eastern tip of the United States, were the scene of many wrecks over the years, although few involved loss of life. A lifesaving station, one of a dozen on the Maine coast, was established at Carrying Place Cove, near West Quoddy Head, in 1874.

In an article in *Down East* magazine, Philip Searles, grandson of Ephraim Johnson, keeper at West Quoddy Head Lighthouse, described a memorable day in 1929, when Searles was visiting with his grandparents. During breakfast, word arrived that a ship had gone aground in thick fog about a mile south of the lighthouse. Johnson called the local Coast Guard station, and he soon followed the assistant keeper, Eugene Larrabee, who ran down the shoreline with a supply of rope.

Arriving at the scene of the disaster, Searles saw a two-masted ship stuck in a crevice in the rocky cliff. Larrabee and another man were able to get a line to the vessel, and the crewmen climbed one at a time onto the rocks, After the men were safely rescued, the ship slid off the rocks and within minutes had sunk out of sight, except for the tips of the masts.

THE LAST FOUR-MASTED schooner built in Canada, the *Whitebelle,* from New Brunswick, ran onto the rocks at Gulliver's Hole in Lubec on May 22, 1931. On impact the vessel broke in half, and much of the coal it was carrying was dumped into the ocean.

Gulliver's Hole, which is about a half mile from West Quoddy Head Lighthouse, was long rumored to be the hiding place of pirate treasure. One keeper's son dug extensively and enthusiastically, but all he found was an occasional bottle or anchor chain.

THE *Castine,* a sixty-five-foot excursion steamer built in 1889, was passing near the Inner Bay Ledges, off Vinalhaven, in thick fog on the morning of June 8, 1935. The seventy-five passengers, most of them members of local granges, had boarded the boat in Belfast and were headed for Vinalhaven, where there was to be a picnic with grange members on the island.

The vessel began to strike the ledges, and Captain Leighton Coombs ordered the engines stopped. The steamer was soon tipping to one side, sending passengers over the side into Penobscot Bay. Seawater struck the boilers, sending clouds of steam surging into the air. Many vessels responded quickly to a distress signal from the *Castine,* including the steamer *North Haven* and several lobster boats.

Four people died in the accident, and the rest were rescued. Among the passengers was ninety-year-old Colonel Fernando S. Philbrick, a veteran of the Civil War. When the steamer hit the ledge, Philbrick fell to the floor and was pinned under a chair. He watched helplessly as other passengers threw ropes to those who had fallen overboard. A woman, Grace Packard of Camden, lay across Philbrick's legs. "I thought she was dead," he said later. "I brushed back her hair and wiped the water from her face."

When help arrived, Captain Coombs pleaded with Philbrick to get on board one of the rescue boats. He refused to leave until Packard was rescued. According to witnesses, Philbrick shouted, "Get the woman first. I'm all right. I can hold out here for a long time yet." Philbrick was taken to a local hospital, where he recovered.

The *Castine* broke in two and was a complete loss. The forward quarter was salvaged; it was taken to Cedar Island, near Vinalhaven, where it was turned upside down and served as a guesthouse near a log cabin.

According to Roy Heisler of the Vinalhaven Historical Society, "A firsthand story of the 'summer camp' fashioned from the wreck of the *Castine* was recently related by a retired carpenter who repaired it many years ago. He said the owner of the island kept it open in the winter, stocked with canned goods and with heat in case it was needed in any emergency, possibly meaning other wrecks."

TWO OF THE LAST, proud, four-masted schooners came to a sad end on the waterfront of Wiscasset, Maine, late in the twentieth century. They weren't wrecked by a storm; this was a slow demolition by neglect. The ships were the *Luther Little* and the *Hesper*, built in Somerset, Massachusetts, in 1917 and 1918, respectively. Both of the majestic schooners were more than two hundred feet long.

The *Little* and the *Hesper* had short careers at sea as the days of sailing ships waned. They ended up abandoned, next to each other, near the Wiscasset end of the bridge crossing the Sheepscot River. In that location, they were visited and photographed by thousands of tourists until their rotting remains were hauled away in 1998.

Selected Bibliography

Bachelder, Peter Dow. *Shipwrecks and Maritime Disasters of the Maine Coast.* Portland, Maine: Provincial Press, 1997.

Buker, George E. *The Penobscot Expedition.* Annapolis: Naval Institute Press, 2002.

Caldwell, Bill. *Islands of Maine.* Portland, Maine: Guy Gannett, 1981.

Cape Elizabeth: Past to Present. Cape Elizabeth, Maine: Town of Cape Elizabeth, 1991.

Cutler, Carl C. *Greyhounds of the Sea.* New York: Halcyon House, 1930.

D'Entremont, Jeremy. *The Lighthouses of Maine.* Beverly, Mass.: Commonwealth Editions, 2009.

Ellms, Charles. *The Tragedy of the Seas.* Philadelphia: C. Sherman, 1841.

Jordan, William, Jr. *A History of Cape Elizabeth, Maine.* 1965. Reprint, Bowie, Md.: Heritage Books, 1987.

Keatts, Henry. *New England's Legacy of Shipwrecks.* Kings Point, N.Y.: American Merchant Marine Museum Press, 1988.

Kingston, W. H. G. *John Deane of Nottingham.* 1879. Reprint, London: Tutis Digital Publishing, 2008.

Mason, John. "The Wreck of the *Royal Tar.*" In *Yankees under Steam,* edited by Austin N. Stevens. Dublin, N.H.: Yankee, 1970.

McLane, Charles B. *Islands of the Mid-Maine Coast: Blue Hill Bay.* Woolwich, Maine: Kennebec River Press, 1985.

———. *Islands of the Mid-Maine Coast: Muscongus Bay and Monhegan Island.* Gardiner, Maine: Tilbury House, 1992.

———. *Islands of the Mid-Maine Coast: Pemaquid Point to the Kennebec River.* Gardiner and Rockland, Maine: Tilbury House and Island Institute, 1994.

———. *Islands of the Mid-Maine Coast: Penobscot Bay.* 1982. Reprint, Gardiner and Rockland, Maine: Tilbury House and Island Institute, 1997.

———. *Islands of the Mid-Maine Coast, Volume II: Mount Desert to Machias Bay*. Falmouth, Maine: Kennebec River Press, 1989.

Meryman, William Ernest. *The Wind Blew and the Ship Flew*. Newell, Iowa: Bireline, 1982.

Moody, Kenneth A. *Golden State/Annie C. Maguire*. Published by the author, 2001.

Nash, Gilbert. *The Original Journal of General Solomon Lovell, Kept during the Penobscot Expedition, 1779, With a Sketch of His Life*. 1881. Reprint, Whitefish, Mont.: Kessinger, 2009.

Paine, Ralph D. *Lost Ships and Lonely Seas*. New York: Century, 1921.

Parker, Gail Underwood. *It Happened in Maine*. Guilford, Conn.: Globe Pequot Press, 2004.

Perley, Sidney. *Historic Storms of New England*. 1891. Reprint, Beverly, Mass.: Commonwealth Editions, 2001.

Puleo, Stephen. *Due to Enemy Action*. Guilford, Conn.: Lyons Press, 2005.

Quinn, William P. *Shipwrecks along the Atlantic Coast*. 1988. Reprint, Beverly, Mass.: Commonwealth Editions, 2004.

———. *Shipwrecks around Maine*. Orleans, Mass.: Lower Cape Publishing, 1983.

Riess, Warren C. *Angel Gabriel: The Elusive English Galleon*. Bristol, Maine: 1797 House, 2001.

Roberts, Kenneth, Jack Bales, and Richard Warner, editors. *Boon Island, Including Contemporary Accounts of the Wreck of the Nottingham Galley*. Hanover, N.H.: University Press of New England, 1996. (Roberts's novel *Boon Island* was originally published by Doubleday, 1956.)

Roerden, Chris. *Collections from Cape Elizabeth, Maine*. Cape Elizabeth, Maine: Town of Cape Elizabeth, 1965.

Rowe, William Hutchinson. *The Maritime History of Maine*. New York: W. W. Norton, 1948.

Roy, M. Chris. *The Wiscasset Ships*. Westport Island, Maine: Pumpkin Press, 1994.

Shanks, Ralph, and Wick York. *The U.S. Life-Saving Service*. Edited by Lisa Woo Shanks. Petaluma, Calif.: Costaño Books, 1996.

Snow, Edward Rowe. *Fantastic Folklore and Fact*. New York: Dodd, Mead, 1968.

———. *Great Storms and Famous Shipwrecks of the New England Coast*. New York: Dodd, Mead, 1943.

———. *Marine Mysteries and Dramatic Disasters of New England*. New York: Dodd, Mead, 1976.

———. *New England Sea Tragedies*. New York: Dodd, Mead, 1960.

———. *The Romance of Casco Bay*. New York: Dodd, Mead, 1975.

———. *Strange Tales from Nova Scotia to Cape Hatteras*. New York: Dodd, Mead, 1949.

———. *True Tales of Terrible Shipwrecks*. New York: Dodd, Mead, 1963.

———. *The Vengeful Sea*. New York: Dodd, Mead, 1956.

Snow, Wilbert. "Fate of the *Royal Tar*." In *Yankees under Steam,* edited by Austin N. Stevens. Dublin, N.H.: Yankee, 1970.

Sterling, Robert Thayer. *Maine Lighthouses and the Men Who Keep Them*. Brattleboro, Vt.: Stephen Daye Press, 1935.

Welner, Stacy L. *Tragedy in Casco Bay*. Harpswell, Maine: Anchor Publishing, 2006.

Willard, Benjamin J. *Captain Ben's Book*. Portland, Maine: Lakeside Press, 1895.

Web Sites

Hunting New England Shipwrecks, www.wreckhunter.net

Maine Memory Network, www.mainememory.net

Index

Page numbers given in *italics* indicate illustrations or material contained in their captions.

111

CPSIA information can be obtained
at www.ICGtesting.com
Printed in the USA
BVHW07s2017040618

518175BV00001B/16/P